THE IMPROBABLE CONQUEST

THE IMPROBABLE CONQUEST

Sixteenth-Century Letters from the Río de la Plata

Edited and translated by
Pablo García Loaeza and Victoria L. Garrett

The Pennsylvania State University Press
University Park, Pennsylvania

Library of Congress Cataloging-in-Publication Data

The improbable conquest : sixteenth-century letters
from the Río de la Plata / edited and translated by
Pablo García Loaeza and Victoria L. Garrett.
    pages   cm—(Latin American originals ; 9)
Summary: "A translation of letters written by settlers
in the Río de la Plata region of South America during
the Spanish conquest in the sixteenth century"—
Provided by publisher.
Includes bibliographical references and index.
ISBN 978-0-271-06548-9 (pbk. : alk. paper)
1. Río de la Plata Region (Argentina and Uruguay)—
Discovery and exploration—Spanish.
2. Río de la Plata Region (Argentina and Uruguay)—
History—16th century.
3. Spaniards—Río de la Plata Region (Argentina and
Uruguay)—History—16th century.
4. Spaniards—Río de la Plata Region (Argentina and
Uruguay)—Correspondence.
5. Explorers—Spain—Correspondence.
I. Loaeza, Pablo García, 1972– , editor, translator.
II. Garrett, Victoria L. (Victoria Lynn), 1981– , editor,
translator. III. Series: Latin American originals ; 9.

F2909.I47 2015
916.3'68—dc23
2014028301

CONTENTS

Foreword / vii

Preface / xi

Acknowledgments / xv

Chronology / xvii

Introduction / 1

Selected Letters from the Río de la Plata / 29

    Pedro de Mendoza to Juan de Ayolas (April 21, 1537) / 29

    Isabel de Guevara to Princess Juana (July 2, 1556) / 34

    Domingo de Irala to Emperor Charles V (March 1, 1545) / 43

    Francisco Galán to Rodrigo de Vera (March 1, 1545) / 54

    Juan Pavón to Martín de Agreda (June 15, 1556) / 61

    Francisco de Andrada to the Council of the Indies (March 1, 1545) / 65

    Martín González to Emperor Charles V (June 25, 1556) / 76

    Domingo Martínez to Emperor Charles V (July 2, 1556) / 92

Epilogue / 101

Glossary of Spanish Terms / 105

Bibliography / 109

Index / 113

Latin American Originals (LAO) is a series of primary source texts on colonial Latin America. LAO volumes are accessible, affordable editions of texts translated into English—most of them for the very first time. Of the nine volumes now in print, six illuminate aspects of the Spanish conquests during the long century of 1494–1614, and three push our understandings of the spiritual conquest into surprising new territories.

Taken in the chronological order of their primary texts, LAO 7 comes first. *Of Cannibals and Kings* presents the very earliest written attempt to describe the native cultures of the Americas. The volume combines the early ethnography by the Catalan Ramón Pané with Spanish accounts of Caribbean societies of the late 1490s. Together they offer striking new insight into how the first Europeans in the Americas struggled from the very start to conceive a New World.

Following the chronological sequence of the sources, LAO 2 comes next. *Invading Guatemala* shows how reading multiple accounts of conquest wars (in this case, Spanish, Nahua, and Maya versions of the Guatemalan conflict of the 1520s) can explode established narratives and suggest a conquest story that is more complicated, disturbing, and revealing. LAO 1, *Invading Colombia*, challenges us to view the difficult Spanish invasion of Colombia in the 1530s as more representative of conquest campaigns than the better-known assaults on the Aztec and Inca empires.

This latest volume in the series, LAO 9, takes us further into the sixteenth century and south to the region that would eventually become Argentina. In *The Improbable Conquest* expert translators and editors Pablo García Loaeza and Victoria L. Garrett have chosen letters written by the Spaniards who tried to found a colony along the hopefully named Río de la Plata. The eight missives, penned between 1537 and 1556, reveal so well the trials and tribulations of those efforts that the persistence of the colonists seems improbable indeed.

LAO 3, *The Conquest on Trial*, features a fictional embassy of native Americans filing a complaint over the conquest in a court in Spain—the Court of Death. That text, the first theatrical examination of the conquest published in Spain, effectively condensed contemporary debates on colonization into one dramatic package. LAO 4, *Defending the Conquest*, is a spirited, ill-humored, and polemic apologia for the Spanish Conquest written by Bernardo de Vargas Machuca, a lesser-known veteran conquistador, submitted for publication—without success—in 1613.

Volumes 5, 6, and 8 all explore aspects of Spanish efforts to implant Christianity in the New World. LAO 6, *Gods of the Andes*, presents the first English edition of a 1594 manuscript describing Inca religion and the campaign to convert native Andeans. Its Jesuit author, Blas Valera, is surprisingly sympathetic to preconquest beliefs and practices, viewing them as preparing Andeans for the arrival of the faith he helped bring from Spain. LAO 5, *Forgotten Franciscans*, casts new light on the spiritual conquest and the conflictive cultural world of the Inquisition in sixteenth-century Mexico. LAO 5 and 6 both show how there were wildly divergent views within the church in Spanish America both on native religions and on how to replace them with Christianity. Beautifully complementing those two volumes, by revealing the indigenous side of the same process, is LAO 8. In *Translated Christianities* Mark Christensen presents religious texts translated from Nahuatl and Yucatec Maya. Designed to proselytize and ensure the piety of indigenous parishioners in Central Mexico and Yucatan, these texts show how such efforts actually contributed to the development of local Christianities. As in other parts of the Americas, native cultures thrived within the conversion process, leading to fascinatingly multifaceted outcomes.

The source texts to LAO volumes are either colonial-era rare books or archival documents—written in European languages or in indigenous ones, such as Nahuatl and Maya. The contributing authors are historians, anthropologists, and scholars of literature; they have developed a specialized knowledge that allows them to locate, translate, and present these texts in a way that contributes to scholars' understanding of the period, while also making them readable for students and nonspecialists. Pablo García Loaeza and Victoria L. Garrett are just such scholars. Both hold doctorates and teach classes in Spanish literature, with broad and complementary specializations in various aspects of Latin American culture—from conquest literature to the origins of patriotism to popular theater—helping them to make this unique and resonant contribution to the LAO series.

—Matthew Restall

No Spanish fleet sailed to the New World without a designated notary charged with keeping an official record of every episode of a *conquista*. They chronicled routes taken, decisions made, and sentences passed together with their consequences. They noted major and minor details about the weather, the landscape, and the natives they encountered in their journeys. Additionally, everyone felt entitled to write to the authorities. Even in the most remote locations and the direst of straits, the Spanish conquistadors took pen to paper in order to document their actions. They knew they would eventually rely on written accounts to claim rewards for their service, denounce injustices suffered, or justify their own misconduct. It may even be said that their sense of belonging to a civilized society was maintained through writing. Thus, there is an extensive collection of letters written by assorted individuals about the conquest of the New World. They constitute an unofficial record of the colonial enterprise and offer an insider's point of view of its challenges and hardships.

This selection of sixteenth-century letters from the Río de la Plata provides rare insight into an improbable conquest, an endeavor that tottered on the brink of failure for two decades. From 1536 to 1556, the first settlers of the region were constantly beset by misfortune and plagued by ceaseless infighting. Every time they could, they addressed their woes, their complaints, and their hopes to remote authorities in Spain, exposing the unglamorous side of the conquest. Written by all manner of persons, these texts constitute an underappreciated resource, both as historical documents and as rhetorical artifacts—the tension between these two facets is just one of many topics worthy of further exploration.

A long series of hardships and frustrations prompted the protagonists of this conquest to write. In 1537, Pedro de Mendoza, the first governor[1] and *adelantado* of the Río de la Plata, wrote to his lieutenant, Juan de Ayolas. He advised him, among other things, to be wary of certain people who might plot treason, recommending that he judge them fairly if he could find enough evidence to put them on trial, or dispose of them discreetly if he could not. The *adelantado* himself was preparing to sail back to Spain after a series of mishaps that had reduced an exceptionally well-outfitted expedition to abject misery in less than a year. Ayolas never got the letter; he had disappeared into the jungle forevermore. Ayolas's second in command, the controversial Domingo Martínez de Irala, took over leadership of the colony. The situation did not improve much. In 1541, the original settlement of Buenos Aires was abandoned, and the colonists relocated upriver to Asunción. The following year, the famous castaway Álvar Núñez Cabeza de Vaca reached the new settlement to assume the post of governor and second *adelantado*. However, he was unable to impose his authority and was removed from power in 1544. The same ship that transported Cabeza de Vaca back to Spain in 1545 carried letters in which the colonists relayed the turbulent events leading up to his arrest and commented on the colony's situation. In 1556, after the crown had formally recognized Irala as governor, his detractors wrote to complain about the injustices they had suffered and the abuses perpetrated against the natives during his time as acting governor. Irala's death in late 1556 ended the controversy and marked the end of the first stage of the Río de la Plata conquest. Full of passion, conflict, and strife, the captivating history of this venture truly comes alive in the letters written by the people who lived through it.

1. In the New World's frontiers, trailblazing governors were often the highest civil authority. These governors could distribute land and assign *encomiendas*. To keep governors from establishing themselves as feudal lords, the crown limited the duration of their terms in office to a few years.

The Río de la Plata. Map by Maria Panaccione and Pablo García.

ACKNOWLEDGMENTS

We are deeply indebted to Teresa Méndez-Faith for pointing the
way to Paraguay. We would also like to thank Matthew Restall and
Ellie Goodman for their encouragement and support. The H-LatAm
Discussion Network generously provided useful bibliographic references; in particular, Dot Tuer kindly shared her doctoral dissertation.
The comments of Edward Chauca, Kris Lane, and N. David Cook
were extremely valuable for revising various versions of the book's
manuscript.

1516	February	Juan Díaz de Solís officially discovers the Río de la Plata region for the Spanish crown.
	March	The natives kill Díaz de Solís.
1520	October	Ferdinand Magellan discovers a passage between the Atlantic and Pacific Oceans.
1526		Disregarding his charge to travel to the Moluccas (aka the Spice Islands) by way of the Strait of Magellan, Sebastian Cabot explores the Río de la Plata.
1527	February	Sebastian Cabot establishes a fort named Sancti Spíritus near the Paraná River.
1528	February	On his way to the Pacific, Diego García de Moguer reaches the Río de la Plata; he meets Cabot and agrees to join his explorations.
1529	September	The natives attack and raze Sancti Spíritus.
1530		Cabot and García de Moguer reach Spain.
1532		Preparations for a new expedition to the Río de la Plata begin.
1534	May	Pedro de Mendoza negotiates his *capitulación* with the Spanish crown.
1535	August	Mendoza's fleet sails from Spain toward the Río de la Plata.
	December	En route to the Río de la Plata, Juan Osorio is killed on Mendoza's orders for alleged sedition.
1536	February	Mendoza reaches the Río de Plata and establishes Buenos Aires.
	March	Juan de Ayolas sets out to explore the Paraguay River.
	June 15	First major battle between conquistadors and natives.

	June 15	Ayolas establishes the fort at Corpus Christi; leaving a few people to man the fort, he turns back to help those in Buenos Aires.
	September	Pedro de Mendoza establishes the fort at Buena Esperanza, midway between Buenos Aires and Corpus Christi.
	October	Ayolas goes further up the Paraguay River, while Mendoza goes back to Buenos Aires.
1537	January	Juan de Salazar goes in search of Ayolas.
	February	Ayolas names the port of La Candelaria (February 2), appoints Domingo de Irala as his lieutenant, and disappears inland.
	April	Pedro de Mendoza sets sail for Spain; he leaves a deed designating Ayolas as his lieutenant governor and Francisco Ruiz Galán as commander in Buenos Aires.
	June	Mendoza dies at sea.
	August 15	Juan de Salazar establishes the fort of Asunción.
1538	November	The *veedor* Alonso Cabrera reaches Buenos Aires with instructions to ascertain the governorship of the Río de la Plata.
1539	May	Cabrera officially recognizes Irala as governor.
1540	December	Álvar Núñez Cabeza de Vaca, designated governor and second *adelantado* of the Río de la Plata, sails from Spain.
1541	March	Cabeza de Vaca's fleet reaches the island of Santa Catalina.
	June	The settlement at Buenos Aires is dismantled and abandoned.
	November	Cabeza de Vaca sets out toward Asunción by land with half his force, while the rest sail on toward Buenos Aires.
1542	March	Cabeza de Vaca reaches Asunción and assumes the governorship.
1543	September	Cabeza de Vaca undertakes an *entrada* up the Paraguay River.
1544	March	The *entrada* is thwarted by general sickness and the royal officials' schemes; Cabeza de Vaca has no choice but to return to Asunción.
	April	Cabeza de Vaca is arrested.
1545	March	Cabeza de Vaca is sent back to Spain.

1547		Irala begins another expedition to seek the Sierra de la Plata, leaving Francisco de Mendoza as commander in Asunción.
1548	September	Having reached Peruvian territory, Irala sends Nuflo de Chávez with messages for the Spanish authorities in Lima.
	November	Chávez reaches Lima. Irala is deposed; the royal officials designate Gonzalo de Mendoza as commander for the return to Asunción. Meanwhile, in Asunción, Francisco de Mendoza had relinquished power to Diego de Abreu, who then had Mendoza beheaded.
1549	March	The returning expedition receives the news of the developments in Asunción; Irala is once again designated as commander.
	April	Irala enters Asunción; Abreu is arrested but manages to escape soon after.
1552	November	The crown finally decides to appoint Irala as governor.
1553	January	Irala undertakes a new expedition in search of legendary riches; left in command at Asunción, Felipe de Cáceres pursues Diego de Abreu.
	September	Irala returns to Asunción.
1555	August	Irala officially receives the title of governor of the Río de la Plata.
1556		Governor Irala allocates *encomiendas* to the settlers.
	April	Bishop Pedro Fernández de la Torre arrives in Asunción.
	October	Domingo Martínez de Irala dies.

Introduction

Over the past two decades, historians have paid little attention to sixteenth-century Río de la Plata.[1] As Dorothy Tuer (2011, 23) judiciously explains, the prominence of Buenos Aires, the ongoing controversies surrounding *Peronismo*, and the tragic legacy of the 1976–83 military dictatorship have kept the focus of recent Argentine historiography on the twentieth century. Meanwhile, academic research in Paraguay has been mired by centuries of political repression that resulted in the country's isolation and impoverishment.[2] Moreover, the demarcation of history along modern national borders has gotten in the way of a comprehensive consideration of the region's early colonial period.[3] The current lack of interest is disconcerting in view of the history's significance, its dramatic appeal, and a rich archive of documents and primary sources.

Other than the many legal documents, the historiographic sources for the early history of the Río de la Plata include the eyewitness account of the German mercenary Ulrich Schmidl (Schmidel, Schmidt), first published in 1567 in a travel collection as *Warhafftige und liebliche Beschreibung erstlicher furnemen Indianischen Landtschafften und Insulen, die vormals in keiner Chronicken gedacht, und erstlich in der Schiffart Ulrici Schmidts von Straubingen, mit grosser gefahr erkundigt, und von ihmselber auffs fleissigst*

---

1. Scholars have been more drawn to the seventeenth century and the missionizing efforts of the Jesuits among the Guaraní. The appeal comes from the social order established in the missions, which has been described as utopian, as well as from the wealth of ethnographic materials produced by the missionaries. For a recent assessment of the Jesuit missions in Paraguay see Ganson 2005.

2. It is symptomatic that in 2011 the Paraguayan studies section of the Latin American Studies Association was closed due to lack of membership.

3. Tellingly, for historian Efraím Cardozo (1959) colonial Paraguay seems to overlay the modern state's borders, which leaves out much of the original span of the Río de la Plata province.

beschrieben und dargethan (True and delightful description of some Indian lands and islands that have never been mentioned before in any chronicle, first explored at great risk in the seafaring exploration of Ulrich Schmidl of Straubing, and recorded and meticulously described by him).[4] For the governorship of Álvar Núñez Cabeza de Vaca, his own *Comentarios* (1555) present a detailed but biased narrative. They are complemented by the *Relación de las cosas sucedidas en el Río de la Plata* written in 1545 by Pero Hernández, who was Cabeza de Vaca's secretary. Consequently, his account is partial to Cabeza de Vaca and exceedingly inimical to Domingo Martínez de Irala. In the early seventeenth century, Ruy Díaz de Guzmán, the grandson of one of the original conquistadors, wrote *La Argentina*, a history that covers the years 1514 to 1573 and is based partly on the testimony of some of the story's actors. It was not published until the nineteenth century.

In the 1930s, based on extensive archival research, the Argentine historian Enrique de Gandía published several books on the Río de la Plata's early colonial period. Though some of Gandía's interpretations manifest outdated prejudices, his erudite texts reflect a magisterial knowledge of the primary sources; in terms of the sequence of events and amount of detail, they remain unsurpassed. The following narrative, which owes much to Gandía's work, provides the reader with a general historical overview, offering a framework for reading the letters individually and as a set.

The Exploration, Conquest, and Early Colonization of the Río de la Plata

THE SOUTHERN PASSAGE AND THE SIERRA DE LA PLATA

The European discovery of America came on the heels of intense competition between the Spanish and the Portuguese for maritime dominance. In 1493, Pope Alexander VI divided the terrestrial globe between the kingdoms of Castile and Portugal. The bull (papal decree) known as *Inter caetera* limited the range of Portuguese transatlantic activity to 100 leagues west of the Azores islands; any lands

---

4. In 1891, the Hakluyt Society published an English translation of Schmidl's account by Luis Domínguez (2010). Though dated, it remains the only one.

discovered beyond that would belong to the crown of Castile. A year later, the treaty signed at Tordesillas pushed the boundary farther west, setting it at 370 leagues from the Cape Verde islands. However, the lack of precise coordinates and measurements made it impossible to establish the divide's exact location. As a result, Castile and Portugal engaged in a furious race to gain an advantageous position in contested areas. In particular, Castile laid claim to the spice-rich Moluccas islands in the Mar del Sur, later known as the Pacific Ocean. In order to strengthen its case, the Castilian crown sought to reach them by sailing west through a not yet discovered southern passage cutting across the New World.

In 1514, Juan Díaz de Solís agreed to set out in search of the passage between the Atlantic Ocean, known as the Mar del Norte, and the Mar del Sur.[5] Three caravels sailed from Sanlúcar de Barrameda on October 8, 1515. In early 1516, the fleet reached what Díaz de Solís called the Mar Dulce, the estuary that would later be called Río de la Plata. The brief exploration of this promising "sweet-water sea" ended when the natives attacked, killed, and allegedly devoured a landing party led by Díaz de Solís. Suddenly left without a leader, the expedition's lieutenants decided that the best course of action was to go back to Spain. However, one of the ships ran aground. Some of the survivors remained near the shipwreck, others traveled up the coast to seek help from Portuguese traders,[6] and a few more journeyed far inland. The latter group was led by Alejo García, whose name was often mentioned as a geographic and temporal reference by later explorers of the region.

The southern passage was found in 1520 by Ferdinand Magellan, who named the Pacific Ocean after crossing the straight that bears his name. Two years later, after completing the first circumnavigation

---

5. Two years earlier, Díaz de Solís was to lead a secret voyage intended the reach the Moluccas from the west by sailing around Africa. Portugal discovered and objected strongly to the project, which was cancelled as a result. In 1513, Vasco Núñez de Balboa's discovery of the Mar del Sur across the Isthmus of Panama stimulated the search for a sea passage from one ocean to the other.

6. Brazil was officially discovered for the Portuguese crown by Pedro Álvares Cabral in 1500. Portugal was engaged in very profitable oriental trade and, other than trying to prevent piracy, paid little heed to its transatlantic territory. A few *feitorias*, or trading posts, were established on the coast to acquire brazilwood. Sustained efforts to colonize Brazil did not begin in earnest until the 1530s, and their progress was very slow.

of the globe, the lone ship that managed to return to Spain brought news of the discovery. The Moluccas still represented a point of contention. A new Spanish expedition to reach the islands by way of the Strait of Magellan was quickly organized; it left Spain in 1525.[7] Soon after, Spain signed a contract with Sebastian Cabot, who was to sail due west in order to conduct further explorations in the Far East. In 1526, Cabot reached the southern coast of Brazil, where he heard stories of a land of riches accessible by the Río de Solís (as the Río de la Plata was then called). Cabot abandoned his original goal and sailed up the Paraná River, going as far as the junction with the Paraguay River. On the way, he established the first European settlement in the region, the fort of Sancti Spíritus, in 1527.[8]

In 1528, on his return from the Paraguay, Cabot ran into Diego García de Moguer at Sancti Spíritus. Like Cabot, García de Moguer had been en route to the Moluccas, but resolved to seek the rumored silver-rich Sierra de la Plata instead. The two men agreed to join forces. However, it was not long before the lack of supplies and destruction of the fort by natives persuaded them to sail back to Spain. They arrived in 1530 with a few silver samples and many alluring stories about all the precious metal that could be found by sailing up the river that became known as the Río de la Plata.

Preparations to establish a permanent Spanish presence in the area and thus facilitate the quest for the fabled Sierra de la Plata began in 1532. The arrival in Spain of Atahualpa's kingly ransom of gold and silver in January 1534 lent greater urgency to the project.[9] In May of that year, Pedro de Mendoza was officially designated as *adelantado*, or military commander, and governor of the Río de la Plata. Mendoza's credentials included a noble lineage, a long record of service, and membership in the prestigious knightly Order of Santiago. Moreover, his considerable wealth allowed him to finance a large portion of the undertaking. In return, Mendoza obtained generous allowances from

7. Only one of the seven ships that made up the fleet commanded by García Jofre de Loaisa managed to reach its destination a year later.

8. Sancti Spíritus was located somewhere near the town of Gaboto in present-day Argentina.

9. Seeking to emulate Hernán Cortés's success in Mexico, Francisco Pizarro detained the Inca ruler Atahualpa in late 1532. Hoping to regain his freedom, Atahualpa gave a great amount of gold and silver to Pizarro who, nonetheless, had him executed a few months later.

the crown. Among other things, he was promised the title of count and ten thousand vassals within his governorship.

Dreams of vast wealth drove many would-be conquistadors to sign up for the voyage to the Río de la Plata. As a result, Mendoza's fleet was one of the largest to ever set sail for the New World. Around fifteen hundred men and women from diverse walks of life and various nationalities departed on eleven ships from Sanlúcar de Barrameda on August 24, 1535. Three more ships joined the fleet in the Canary Islands, the last stop before the ocean crossing.

DISCORD, DEARTH, AND DESPAIR

The journey to the New World was not without incident. At the stop in the Canary Islands, Jorge de Mendoza secretly brought a girl on board, meaning to sail away with her. The next day a storm forced the fleet to return to port only to find a group of angry islanders willing to open fire on the ships. Eventually, the ship's captain and the island's governor settled the matter of the abduction. Since the union had already been consummated, it was agreed that the couple should marry immediately. Leaving the newlyweds behind, the fleet sailed on. One of the ships veered off course and never caught up to the group that set out with Mendoza. Instead, it sailed north to Santo Domingo and from there to Spain. Gandía estimates that the loss of that particular ship, which was carrying important provisions and tools, determined much of what happened afterward.[10] Another noteworthy event was Juan Osorio's execution. Osorio, who was apparently well liked by everyone, was accused of planning a mutiny. An inquiry into the matter was conducted in secret. Governor Mendoza found him guilty and sentenced him to death. A short time later, Osorio was seized and stabbed. His body was left unburied with a sign that, perhaps unjustly, proclaimed him a traitor.[11] This unsavory

10. According to Gandía (1936b, 12), Mendoza decided to remain in Buenos Aires in order to wait for the well-laden ship. The *Santiago* was commanded by Alonso Cabrera, who upon returning to the Río de la Plata as *veedor* played a decisive role in the rise to power of Domingo de Irala in 1539, the desertion of Buenos Aires in 1541, and the deposition of Álvar Núñez Cabeza de Vaca in 1544.

11. Upon learning of Osorio's death in 1537, his father, Juan Vásquez de Orejón, presented a suit at the Council of the Indies to have his name cleared of the charge of treason. In 1544, the Council sided with the claimant and pronounced that Mendoza had misjudged Osorio.

affair foreshadowed the complications that would plague the colonists over the course of two decades.

Pedro de Mendoza finally disembarked at the Río de la Plata in early February 1536 and established a settlement he named Santa María del Buen Aire, after a well-known patroness of sailors.[12] The colonists soon found themselves in serious trouble. Hunger was of particular concern, and several parties were dispatched in search of food. At one point, Mendoza resolved to raid the neighboring natives, which had disastrous consequences. The settlement was besieged and the colonists were reduced to eating their shoes and, in some cases, one another. The German mercenary Ulrich Schmidl recounts how three Spaniards stole a horse and secretly ate it. When the deed was discovered, they were seized and made to confess under torture. After they had admitted to the crime, they were sentenced to death by hanging; all three were executed. That very night some other Spaniards converged on the three corpses hanging from the gallows; they cut the dead men's thighs and some other pieces of meat and carried them home to satisfy their hunger (Schmidel 1986, 33–34).

Eventually the besiegers withdrew and one of the search crews returned with a few provisions, which gave the colonists a little relief. Meanwhile, Captain Juan de Ayolas had gone beyond the ruins of Cabot's fort at Sancti Spíritus and established an outpost that he named Corpus Christi. He returned to Buenos Aires with some supplies obtained from more welcoming natives. Mendoza decided to accompany Ayolas upriver; a third of those who went along died before reaching Corpus Christi. By this time, the *adelantado* was practically prostrate from his rapidly progressing syphilis.[13] Mendoza left Ayolas, appointed as his lieutenant, to continue exploring upriver while he journeyed back to Buenos Aires by way of a newly established fort at Buena Esperanza.

Mendoza found the settlement at Buenos Aires somewhat more prosperous thanks to the efforts of Francisco Ruiz Galán, who was acting governor, and to supplies obtained in Brazil. After a couple of

---

12. A widespread legend attributes the name to the statement, made by a sailor upon arrival, about the region's good air, or *buen aire*. The precise location of the settlement has been the subject of a protracted and sometimes heated debate.

13. Schmidl (1948, 75) describes Mendoza as being *foller frantzossen*, or full of "French blisters," and unable to move his hands or feet. Also known as "the French disease," syphilis causes rashes, paralysis, dementia, and eventually death.

months, Mendoza dispatched Juan de Salazar to find Ayolas, who had not returned. Two months later, without news from either crew, the ailing *adelantado* opted to return to Spain, effectively abandoning the endeavor. Before leaving, he officially appointed Ayolas as governor and Ruiz Galán as lieutenant governor in his absence. The set of written instructions that Mendoza left for Ayolas, asking him to look after his interests and offering advice on the colony's governance, is included in this volume. Mendoza set sail on April 1537. In June, the first governor and *adelantado* of the Río de la Plata died from his illness and was buried at sea.

THE RISE OF DOMINGO MARTÍNEZ DE IRALA

Meanwhile, Juan de Ayolas had sailed up to the Paraguay River and gone inland at a place he called La Candelaria seeking a way to the Sierra de la Plata. Ayolas's appointed lieutenant, Domingo Martínez de Irala, was to take command of the ships and await his return. Irala did not remain at La Candelaria. Instead, he sailed up- and downriver gathering provisions or, according to his detractors, looking for native women. In June 1537, Juan de Salazar met up with Irala on the Paraguay River. Unable to go after Ayolas or make further progress, the two men went their separate ways: Irala returned to La Candelaria and Salazar went back to the seacoast. On his way downriver, Salazar founded a fort at Santa María de la Asunción[14] among the especially hospitable Guaraní natives. When he finally reached Buenos Aires in October, six months after Pedro de Mendoza's departure, Salazar made his report to Francisco Ruiz Galán, who was poised to assume the governorship. Perhaps in order to assert his authority, Ruiz Galán decided to inspect the newest fort personally, taking everyone from Corpus Christi along with him.

At Asunción, Ruiz Galán found Domingo de Irala. He was there repairing his ships instead of waiting for Juan de Ayolas, whose return he barely missed. According to later reports, Ayolas had managed to retrieve some gold and silver and to make his way back to the

---

14. Juan de Salazar founded Santa María de la Asunción on August 15, 1537. The date corresponds to the feast of the Assumption of the Virgin Mary. According to Catholic tradition, the mother of Christ physically ascended to heaven at the end of her earthly life.

river, only to be killed by the natives. Explanations for the attitude change of the formerly friendly Payaguá differ. Irala's detractors contend that he had offended a Payaguá chieftain by having intercourse with the daughter he had given to Ayolas as a token of allegiance. In the letter included here, Francisco Galán—who is not to be confused with Francisco Ruiz Galán—argues that the Payaguá wanted to keep the riches that Ayolas had found. The only certainty is that Ayolas's fate was sealed by his lieutenant's untimely departure from La Candelaria. The absence of Ayolas resulted in a power struggle between Ruiz Galán and Irala, each alleging the precedence of their claim as next in the line of command.

Matters stood at an impasse until the 1538 arrival of Alonso Cabrera, who had been appointed *veedor* and charged with looking after the crown's interests in the colony. Three years earlier, the fateful Cabrera was on the ship that had sailed with Pedro de Mendoza's fleet but had gotten lost, ending up in Santo Domingo before returning to Spain. In September 1537, after several frustrated attempts to send relief to the colonists at the Río de la Plata,[15] Cabrera took command of two ships bound for Buenos Aires. The news about the colony's struggles discouraged the sailors, many of whom were forced to embark under threat of prison. Cabrera's instructions were to ascertain who would govern, either through Pedro de Mendoza's authority or by popular consent. Much has been made of the royal decree that invited the first electoral experiment in the New World. However, since Cabrera sided with Irala, there was no election at the time. In June 1539, Domingo de Irala walked around the harbor at Asunción and opened the fort's doors as part of the ritual through which he officially assumed the governorship—pending royal ratification.

The new governor's first order of business was to look for Juan de Ayolas, whose death had yet to be conclusively proven. Thinking that Ayolas could still be inland, Irala attempted an *entrada* at the port of San Sebastián, some eight leagues south of La Candelaria. However, the weather and the terrain quickly thwarted the effort.[16] Back at San Sebastián, the searchers met an inland native

---

15. Mendoza's agent and backer in Spain, Martín de Orduña, had bought two ships and supplies to send to the Río de la Plata. However, the ships were not ready by the scheduled departure date of November 1535. Despite pressure from the crown, further unspecified impediments delayed the fleet for two years.

16. West of the Paraguay lies the Gran Chaco, a vast plain that turns from an arid waste in the dry season into a waterlogged quagmire when it rains.

who claimed to have journeyed with Ayolas and who testified to his demise at the hands of the Payaguá. Irala returned to Asunción to fully assume the role of governor.

THE DESERTION OF BUENOS AIRES

The letters by Domingo de Irala and Francisco Galán included in this volume offer contrasting opinions on Irala's first tenure as acting governor. Nevertheless, there can be little doubt that his most consequential decision was to desert Buenos Aires in 1541. Alonso Cabrera, who was in favor of the decision, argued that gathering all the colonists at Asunción would not only preserve them but also facilitate their goal of conquering the Sierra de la Plata. Moreover, it would definitively undercut Ruiz Galán, whose authority in Buenos Aires could challenge Irala's hold on power. On the other hand, abandoning the settlement meant that ships from Spain would find no harbor, while those bound for Spain would have to travel all the way from Asunción. Dissent notwithstanding, Irala had the port dismantled.

In June 1541, the colonists left behind the burning husks of the few buildings that had made up Buenos Aires, including a grounded ship that served as a fortress, and a couple of pigs whose brood might help nourish future expeditionists. Signs and messages were left in various places so that any who came would know to travel upriver, what the best time of the year to undertake the journey was, and what sort of natives they might meet along the way. In order to encourage newcomers, Irala embellished the truth by writing that the Spaniards at Asunción had seven hundred Guaraní women for their service and had amassed significant amounts of silver and gold. Besides endangering the future of the colony, the desertion of Buenos Aires was ill timed: the long-awaited fleet from Spain was just a few miles up the coast, resupplying its stores at the island of Santa Catalina. On board was Álvar Núñez Cabeza de Vaca, the second *adelantado* of the Río de la Plata.

THE SECOND *ADELANTADO*

Álvar Núñez Cabeza de Vaca is well-known for his adventures in the northern frontier of the Spanish New World. After being shipwrecked on the western coast of Florida in 1528, Cabeza de Vaca spent nearly a decade making his way, first by raft and then on foot, to New Spain. Along the journey, he interacted with several different indigenous groups as slave, merchant, or healer. He eventually managed to return to Spain, where he wrote about his experiences. Instead of land or gold, Cabeza de Vaca submitted the narrative itself as a service worthy of recompense from the crown.[17] The gamble was successful. In April 1540, he was named as second *adelantado* and governor of the Río de la Plata. In December, he sailed forth in command of three ships with four hundred men and forty-six horses on board.

The fleet reached the island of Santa Catalina in March 1541, but it was not until November that Cabeza de Vaca, along with about half his men and the surviving horses, set out toward Asunción by land. The remainder of the force was to sail on toward Buenos Aires. It is not hard to imagine the land party's arduous journey across the jungle. However, according to Cabeza de Vaca's account, the natives along the way were extremely welcoming. Reaching the Piquirí River in January 1542, Cabeza de Vaca sent a letter to Asunción requesting assistance to cross the Paraná River. The expected aid never came. Nevertheless, in March 1542, Cabeza de Vaca managed to reach the city and to assume the governorship of the Río de la Plata.

The new arrivals did not constitute the reinforcement that the first-generation colonists had long been awaiting. The hard trek from the coast had depleted Cabeza de Vaca's resources and the residents of Asunción were forced to share what they had with his crew. Moreover, the arrival of a new governor disrupted the existing power structure. In a conciliatory gesture, Cabeza de Vaca named Domingo de Irala as his *maestre de campo,* or second in command. Nonetheless, the new governor's dispositions, which included a review of the colony's accounting and the conquistadors' dealings with the natives, resulted in an increasingly bitter conflict with the veteran commander and the officers who supported him. Matters came to a head in March 1544 when, compelled by the royal officials,[18] Cabeza

---

17. Cabeza de Vaca's *relación* was published in 1542. It was printed again, along with a narrative about his time in the Río de la Plata, in *Naufragios y comentarios* (1555).

18. The royal officials were the *tesorero,* the *contador,* the *factor,* and the *veedor,* who had the joint task of watching over the treasury of a province. In the 1540s, the functions of the *factor* were assumed by the *veedor.* Eventually, the position of *veedor* was also terminated.

de Vaca was forced to quit the *entrada* that they were on and return to Asunción immediately. Just a few days after reaching the city, he was apprehended and put under house arrest. The *adelantado's* supporters were cowed into compliance by those of Domingo de Irala, who reassumed the title of lieutenant governor.

In order to justify the coup, the rebellious officials instigated several judicial inquiries into Cabeza de Vaca's performance as governor. He was accused of tyranny, of substituting the royal coat of arms with his own, and of calling himself sole king of the land. Meanwhile, discord between the two opposing factions simmered. There were many threats, some individual altercations, and a few alleged plots to free the governor until Cabeza de Vaca was taken from his prison, shackled, and put on board a ship bound for Spain in March 1545. And so, with nothing to show for it, the term of the second *adelantado* of the Río de la Plata came to an unhappy end.[19] Before his departure, Cabeza de Vaca designated Juan de Salazar as his lieutenant governor. Salazar made a feeble attempt to assume command, but was almost immediately seized and sent posthaste downriver so that he might join the former governor on his prison ship. The controversies in Asunción, however, were far from over.

REBELS VERSUS *LEALES*

In late 1547, Domingo de Irala organized a new *entrada* in search of the way to the fabled riches of the Sierra de la Plata. Tracing a route from one native group to another, the company traveled as far as the southern reaches of Peru in the fall of 1548. Vexed by finding that he had arrived in already-conquered territory, Irala sent Nuflo de Chávez with dispatches for the authorities in Lima and settled in to await his return.[20] Displeased with the lack of progress and

---

19. It was, however, only the beginning of very lengthy judicial process into the affair. In 1551, the Council of the Indies found Cabeza de Vaca guilty of the charges leveled against him. He was stripped of his titles, banned in perpetuity from the Indies, and sentenced to five years of military service in northern Africa. The former *adelantado* managed to avoid the temporary banishment on appeal and kept litigating for years to recuperate his assets in the Río de la Plata and to have his name and status restored. It is not known whether he achieved the first goal, but there is evidence that he managed the second. See Adorno and Pautz (1999).

20. Chávez finally made his way back to Asunción in late 1550 or early 1551.

intent on going back to Asunción, the royal officials decided to depart
immediately, deposing Irala for the duration of the return journey.
Meanwhile in Asunción, the *leales*, or loyalists—so-called for
their loyalty to former governor Cabeza de Vaca—had wrested
control from Irala's deputy, Francisco de Mendoza, and elected Diego
de Abreu, or d'Abrego, as their leader. Abreu had Mendoza beheaded
as an example for those who would challenge his authority. When
news of this turn of events reached the party returning from Peru,
the royal officials quickly had Irala reinstated as commander. Irala
entered Asunción and quickly arrested Abreu. Abreu managed to
escape but was caught. He escaped again and survived in the wilderness with a few companions for four years before being ambushed
and killed in 1553.

During this period, Irala strove to subdue the *leales* by dispensing
bribes, threats, and death sentences. In one curious instance, he gave
Alonso Riquel de Guzmán and Francisco Ortiz de Vergara, both
leales, a choice between death and marriage to two of his many *mestiza* daughters—they chose the latter. At the same time, Irala sought
to placate the rest of the conquistadors by promising to distribute
land grants among them. However, all major decisions and undertak-
ings were postponed when news about the impending arrival of a
new governor reached Asunción in 1551. A year later, the colonists
were still waiting.[21] Therefore, strife and uncertainty kept prevent-
ing Irala from embarking on a new *entrada*, this time straight to the
north, where rich kingdoms might yet be discovered.

GOVERNOR IRALA

Irala finally set out to explore the upper Paraguay River in early
1553, but the adverse environmental conditions forced him to turn
back after just a few months. This costly and fruitless expedition
became known as the "bad *entrada*." Two years later, Irala's next
attempt was frustrated by the news that the Spanish crown had
finally seen fit to appoint him governor of the Río de la Plata. Irala

21.   The designated governor and third *adelantado* was to be Diego de Sanabria,
the son of Juan de Sanabria, who had received the titles from the crown in 1547 but
had died shortly after. The younger Sanabria finally set sail from Spain 1552 but failed
to reach the Río de la Plata.

officially assumed the post in the summer of 1555. The old quarrels that had long plagued the colony resurfaced. The long-awaited redistribution of the land and natives through *encomiendas* left many discontented.[22] Governor Irala imposed heavy sanctions on anyone who complained about his dealings. Moreover, he decreed restrictions on the circulation of goods and people. The colonists were further irritated by the governor's choice of officers, most of whom were his relatives and allies.

The arrival of the first bishop of the Río de la Plata, Pedro Fernández de la Torre, in the spring of 1556 only contributed to the discord in Asunción. The newly arrived bishop got along well with the governor, but many colonists disliked him, not least for his apparent connivance with Irala. In the summer of 1556, the ship that had brought Bishop de la Torre sailed back to Spain bearing the written complaints and petitions of the people in Asunción. The letters probably had not reached their intended recipients when Domingo de Irala died of a sudden illness in October. His death marked the end of the first and most precarious period of the colonizing effort in the Río de la Plata.

The Guaraní: Friend, Family, and Foe

The improbable conquest of the Río de la Plata would have been altogether impossible had the Spaniards not been integrated into the ethnic landscape of the region through their alliance with the Cario–Guaraní in the area around Asunción.[23] The threadbare band of foreigners that arrived in 1537 did not appear to be a threat to local power dynamics. Rather, the first settlers' survival hinged on their willingness to espouse indigenous cultural norms.

Archeological and linguistic evidence points to the Tupí origin of the Guaraní, who began migrating inland around the year 1000.[24]

22. Necker (1974, 76) suggests that the conquistadors began thinking about becoming *encomenderos* when they failed to find the Sierra de la Plata before reaching Peru in 1548. Roulet (1993, 272) underscores that *encomiendas* were granted much later in the Río de la Plata than elsewhere in the New World and they were minuscule by comparison.

23. This useful insight comes from Florencia Roulet (1993), the main source of the information about the Guaraní provided here.

24. Little is known about Guaraní culture before the early sixteenth century. As Tuer (2011, 30) indicates, its features have been gleaned from comparing colonial

In the early sixteenth century, the core Guaraní area extended from the southern coast of Brazil to the Paraguay River. The Guaraní's neighbors included the agriculturalist Chané near the Andes to the northwest, the Tupí close to the Atlantic coast in the east, and diverse groups of hunter–gatherers, such as the Timbú, the Querandí, and the Charrúa, to the south. On the western side of the Paraguay River, several Guaycurú-speaking groups maintained a relationship of negative reciprocity with the Cario–Guaraní concentrated along the eastern shore that involved periodical raids for women, captives, and revenge.

The Guaraní practiced slash-and-burn agriculture, clearing patches of jungle to grow corn, squash, manioc, beans, and sweet potatoes, and abandoning the fields once the soil that had been temporarily enriched by the burning was spent. Guaraní women planted and harvested the crops. They were also responsible for making pots, weaving baskets, spinning and weaving cotton, as well as gathering firewood and hauling water for cooking. Guaraní men cleared and prepared the planting fields. They were also in charge of hunting, fishing, gathering edible plants and insects, and making canoes, tools, and weapons. Various goods, including wax, honey, animal hides, and *caraguatá* (Bromelia balansae) fiber for weaving and rope making were obtained from the peoples across the river, though trade was contingent on varying levels of interethnic hostility.

Generally, Guaraní communities (*teko'á*) comprised a variable number of households, each an extended family (*teyi*) sharing a single dwelling (*teyi-ogá*). Residence was patrilocal, which meant that married women joined their husbands' households. Marriage entailed obligations toward the wife's family: sons- and brothers-in-law were expected to assist in communal tasks, including hunting and raiding. Only the *tuvichá* was exempt from labor duties toward his in-laws; additionally, he was allowed to have multiple wives and entitled to receive services from the community. Though often identified as a *cacique*, or chief, by the Europeans, the authority of a *tuvichá* did not rest on abstract political notions but on visible traits and concrete deeds: courage, eloquence, and generosity. For instance,

sources, mainly seventeenth- and eighteenth-century Jesuit accounts, with modern fieldwork findings. As in similar cases, the result is a tendency to disregard the dynamism of Guaraní society.

the *tuvichá* was expected to share the surplus of food produced by his wives. Since the title was contingent on an individual's performance, it could be contested and change hands at any time. Solidarity among households and cooperation among communities rested on the peaceful exchange of women through marriage. However, women could also be taken forcibly from different ethnic groups, potentially sparking a revenge cycle. Joint raids were conducted under the leadership of a *mburuvichá*, a great *tuvichá* who exerted his authority over several communities in times of need.[25]

Several features of Guaraní culture account for the peculiarities of the conquest and colonization of the Río de la Plata. Social and linguistic homogeneity facilitated interaction with indigenous communities throughout the region. Specifically, individuals with experience in one region—castaways on the Brazilian coast, for instance—could serve as interpreters and mediators during an *entrada* into uncharted territory (see below). In the beginning, dealings between Spaniards and Guaraní were mutually beneficial. The Spaniards lacked the food that the Guaraní could supply. Likewise, the Guaraní were interested in the Spaniards' metal tools such as iron axes that made it easier to clear land for cultivation. For the Cario–Guaraní in particular, an alliance with the Spaniards, who were quick to draw their steel swords, represented a strategic advantage against their enemies across the river. The Cario sealed the deal by giving women to the Spaniards; the recipients—who became sons- and brothers-in-law—were expected to provide goods and assistance to their indigenous relatives (*tovajá*). As Florencia Roulet (1993, 277) remarks, interethnic relations hinged on Guaraní women, whose many roles—food grower, lover, weaver, mother, cook, and even currency—were vital to both Spaniards and Guaraní.

The Spaniards readily took indigenous women as concubines, but they seldom behaved as dutiful in-laws. The settlers' disregard for the local system of reciprocity was a source of increasing tension. The arrival of Cabeza de Vaca's party in 1542 exacerbated the situation because of the rise in demand for food, women, and services from the indigenous communities around Asunción. Moreover, the new governor's rigid stance regarding the relationship between the Spaniards

---

25. In present-day Paraguay, the presidential residence is called the *Mburuvichá Rogá*, or house of the chief.

and the Guaraní caused not only the civil war that resulted in his ouster but also native uprisings in 1542–43 and 1545–46, when the Spaniards went as far as forming an alliance with the Guaycurú to defend against the Guaraní. Tuer (2011, 256–57) argues that despite continued pressure on the indigenous communities, Domingo de Irala managed to reestablish his authority and maintain the status quo because he was perceived as a powerful and effective *mburuvichá*—at least until 1553, when he led the infamous "bad *entrada*." In 1556, Governor Irala finally agreed to grant the *encomiendas* that settlers had been demanding for years. This new imposition marked the beginning of the colonial period for the region. *Encomiendas* drastically undermined the Guaraní's traditional way of life by restricting mobility, disdaining kinship, and flouting reciprocity. Individuals were not permitted to leave their community or to accept others into their community, trade could only be conducted with the *encomendero*, and women were forbidden from entering into any kind of relationship with a Spaniard.[26]

The *encomienda* system disrupted the indigenous social, political, and economic structures and marked a major change in Spanish–Guaraní relations. However, the system was consistently challenged by the Guaraní, who fled, foiled, or fought their would-be masters until the early seventeenth century. Widespread indigenous insurrections, some lasting for several years, broke out in 1559, 1564, 1568, 1577, 1582, 1584, 1589, 1591, 1592, 1598, 1606, 1610, and 1612.[27] Several revolts involved nativist and religious elements. In one of his letters, dated July 6, 1556, the cleric Martín González wrote about an individual who had "risen up from among the *indios* with a child whom he calls God or the son of God," inspiring the *indios* to sing as they used to in the past. González warned that once the singing started "they [did] not plant or stay in their houses; rather, their only concern was singing and dancing dementedly night and day until they died from hunger and exhaustion, without a single man, woman, child, or old person remaining" (*Cartas* 1877, 632). Later movements had similar traits. They were usually led by a shaman

---

26. A thorough discussion of *encomienda* practices in the Asunción region can be found in Service (1971).

27. Necker (1979, 249–54) provides an annotated inventory of registered insurrections.

(*payé*) who often claimed to have divine powers.[28] These leaders were not necessarily tied to a particular community, but wandered through the region calling for a return to traditional beliefs and practices, preaching against the friars, and in some cases performing de-baptisms. Frenzied dancing and singing were common features, along with the mixing of Guaraní and Christian mythologies and rituals.

Despite recurring resistance, the Guaraní failed to free themselves from colonial impositions. As Roulet (1993, 12) suggests, the slow and gradual progress of the region's colonization veiled the threat that the Spaniards ultimately represented. In the early years, the Guaraní likely thought the conquest of their territory by a few hungry foreigners was improbable at best. Later, their lack of a centralized leadership capable of exercising coercive power prevented a sustained and unified campaign against the colonizers. Even the most extensive insurrections were hampered by long-standing rivalries among the various Guaraní groups as well as the sense of duty that compelled some of them to side with their Spanish relatives by "marriage."

The unions between Spanish men and Guaraní women that initially helped preserve the colony also made possible its expansion through their many *mestizo* children. Even as the Guaraní and Spanish diminished, the mixed-blood population in Asunción increased steadily. Tuer (2011, 310) points out that *mestizos* outnumbered Spaniards five to one at the time of Irala's death in 1556. Eventually, the region's modest economy could not accommodate so many people who were neither *encomenderos* nor *encomendados*. In the second half of sixteenth century, some of these *mestizos* set out to make their fortunes elsewhere. *Mestizo* conquistadors were instrumental in the establishment of new towns and cities including Ciudad Real (1557), Santa Cruz de la Sierra (1561), Villa Rica del Espíritu Santo (1570), and Santa Fe (1573). The port of Buenos Aires was refounded in 1580 with *mestizo* settlers from Asunción. At this time, Franciscan missionaries began gathering the Guaraní in *reducciones*, friar-managed towns that were intended to protect the Guaraní from abuse

28. Rípodas Ardanaz (1987, 262–70) offers an annotated inventory of twenty-four shaman-driven rebellions up to 1660; one was led by a woman who in 1626 claimed to be the mother of God.

and facilitate the work of conversion. This effort set the precedent for the more famous Jesuits missions that, beginning in the seventeenth century, opened a new chapter in colonial Guaraní history.

The Benefit of Experience: Guides and Interpreters

All the expeditions to the Río de la Plata benefited from the experience of individuals who had lived in the region for some time and were familiar with the coastline and the Guaraní language. Some were Portuguese traders. Brazil had been claimed for Portugal in 1500, when Pedro Alvares Cabral accidentally discovered it.[29] Within a decade, Portuguese merchants had established *feitorias*, or trading posts, along the coast to acquire brazilwood and slaves. These stations were instrumental for the Spanish conquest of the Río de la Plata as a haven for castaways, a stop for ships traveling to and from Spain, and a reliable source of supplies. They were also where knowledgeable men could be hired as guides and interpreters. When Sebastian Cabot reached the *feitoria* at Pernambuco in 1526 and, enticed by the tales he heard there, decided to explore the Río de Solís, he took with him the Portuguese Jorge Gomez, who claimed to have been there before. A year later, at the Portuguese port of San Vicente, Diego García de Moguer hired Gonzalo de Acosta to guide his ships to the same river of riches. This was the first of many trips that Acosta would make to the Río de la Plata in the service of Spain.

Gonzalo de Acosta had been in Brazil waiting to collect a shipment of slaves since 1526. In early 1528, he guided García de Moguer to the Río de Solís before returning to San Vicente. In 1530, after García de Moguer abandoned the exploration of the river, Acosta sailed with him back to Spain. In 1534, Emperor Charles V sent a letter to Acosta, addressing him as captain: "Because, having agreed on the terms of the conquest and colonization of the Río de la Plata, Don Pedro de Mendoza is to go to colonize and conquer said land, and because you have some knowledge about that land from having been there, for which you may be of service to us, I command that,

---

29. Alvares Cabral had gone off course: his fleet was bound for India following the route inaugurated by Vasco da Gama, who sailed around Africa to reach Calicut in 1498. Alvares Cabral named his discovery Ilha de Vera Cruz; it came to be called Brazil after the precious wood that was the region's first commodity. See Burns (1993).

immediately after reading this, you prepare yourself to go with the said Don Pedro de Mendoza to the said land" (Medina 1908, 37). Acosta sailed on Mendoza's fleet along with three of his sons. In May 1539, he sailed back to Spain with the delegation commissioned to report on the situation in the Río de la Plata.[30] The following year, Acosta received a letter from the king ordering him to ready himself to return with Álvar Núñez Cabeza de Vaca. When the second *adelantado* decided to travel to Asunción by land, Acosta went along to act as interpreter. In an inquest about his services, Acosta itemized his contributions to the success of the trek. Among other things, Acosta wanted witnesses to certify that "the said Captain Gonzalo Dacosta made all the said *indios* of various places in the said land bring, as they brought, provisions. He was so diligent in doing so that the said crew was well supplied and satisfied all along the said way, . . . owing to the good treatment of the said Gonzalo Dacosta toward the *indios*, and because he compensated them satisfactorily, and because he did not allow them to be mistreated" (Medina 1908, 90–91).

Some of the assertions in Acosta's report seem intentionally self-aggrandizing. However, his ability to mediate between the Spanish and the Guaraní must have been a great asset to Cabeza de Vaca not only on this journey but also during his brief tenure as governor. In 1545, Acosta sailed back to Spain on the same ship as the deposed Cabeza de Vaca. Two years later, Acosta was ordered to join Juan de Sanabria's projected voyage to the Río de la Plata.[31] In 1556, it was Acosta who guided Bishop Pedro de la Torre to Asunción. Finally, in 1557, a letter from King Felipe II instructed Acosta to make ready to sail with Jaime Rasquín, who left Spain in 1559 but never made it to the Río de la Plata.[32] There is no further record of Gonzalo de Acosta, who spent nearly three decades serving as the "on-call" guide for any Spanish expedition bound for the Río de la Plata.[33]

30. The *contador* Felipe de Cáceres was part of this commission. He also sailed back to the Río de la Plata on Cabeza de Vaca's fleet.
31. Juan de Sanabria's death in 1549 thwarted the project. While there is no evidence that Acosta traveled on any of the ships that Sanabria's son and heir, Diego, dispatched to the Río de la Plata, Medina (1908, 72) considers it more than likely.
32. Rasquín's three-ship fleet managed to reach Santo Domingo only to disband there.
33. Acosta's service record is remarkable; however, he was not the only Portuguese employed by Spain. Laguarda (1988, 83) estimates that three quarters of the

The Spanish explorers also profited from the knowledge of sailors from previous expeditions who for various reason had stayed behind. In 1516, one of the ships of the Díaz de Solís fleet ran aground near Los Patos Lagoon. Some of the shipwrecked sailors journeyed up the coast to seek help and passage to Europe from the Portuguese. Others remained in the vicinity of Los Patos living among the natives. A decade later, Sebastian Cabot found two survivors, Enrique Montes and Melchor Ramírez, who confirmed the rumors about the riches that were to be found inland.[34] Cabot took them as his guides. On the river's estuary, another survivor, Francisco del Puerto, joined the expedition.[35] When Cabot decided to sail back to Spain in 1529, not all of his crew left with him. The conquistadors who arrived with Pedro de Mendoza in 1536 benefited from the linguistic and cultural proficiency of some of those veterans, including Hector de Acuña, Juan de Fustes, and Gonzalo Romero. Another of these lingering mariners was Hernando de Ribera, who stands out for having written about his experience. The following excerpts are taken from his letter dated February 25, 1545.[36]

From the outset, Ribera underscores the extent of his experience in matters related to the region, which led to his choice to stay there after Cabot's departure:

> I was already very experienced and knowledgeable of the ways things are in this province. In order to conquer this province, it was necessary to have people on the said coast and island of Santa Catalina so that they could take special care to keep abundant supplies to safeguard, inform, and rescue the ships and people that might reach the island to conquer this land and province. Otherwise, the said conquest would not be feasible without great danger and many lives lost. I decided, in order to

---

ships that sailed to the Río de la Plata over the course of the sixteenth century had Portuguese pilots.

34. A few of the castaways, led by Alejo García, traveled far inland and, before being killed by the natives, managed to send back the samples of precious metals that fueled the legend of the Sierra de la Plata (see Nowell 1946). The story of García and his journey is based exclusively on hearsay and, as Tuer (2011, 56) notes, remains full of uncertainties.

35. Tuer (2011, 69) argues that this individual was not a Spaniard but a baptized native from the Brazilian coast, possibly taken on by Díaz de Solís as an interpreter.

36. Archivo General de Indias, Autos fiscales. Charcas, Justicia, 1131.

serve Your Majesty and so that this province might be conquered, to stay on the said island of Santa Catalina in peace
and harmony with the native *indios*, in order to gather many
stores and the necessary supplies, and to have them ready and
available. And so I stayed in this land for a period of eight years,
waiting for the arrival of people in a fleet with reinforcements
from Your Majesty to conquer this land so as to help them and
join their company in the service of Your Majesty.

It is impossible to know if Ribera's only motive for staying at Santa
Catalina was his wish to serve the king. In any case, his presence
there was useful to the ships that eventually reached the island:

In this time, Don Pedro de Mendoza arrived in this province,
but his fleet did not stop in the ports of Santa Catalina where
we resided. Some time after he had arrived in this province,
he sent a ship to the island of Santa Catalina to gather supplies
to shore up his camp and the people in it. On behalf of Your
Majesty, Mendoza ordered me to come along with the said ship
to help and support the said conquest. As soon as I found out
where he had settled and that his camp was too far away from
the *indios* who could have helped and supported him, I clearly
conceived of the great danger he faced: the injuries and deaths
that awaited him, from both hunger and enemy *indios* from
the said river. Therefore, with great diligence, I had the ship
loaded with supplies and other necessities from the said land.
I embarked on the said ship with my wife, children, slaves, servants, relatives, and friends who were in the said land. I came
to the port of Buenos Aires, which is on the Paraná River and
where the said Don Pedro had settled a town and port.

As Tuer (2011, 100) notes, the considerable entourage that accompanied Ribera to Buenos Aires suggests that he had accumulated a
certain prestige among the natives of Santa Catalina. His bicultural
competence also allowed him to increase his standing among the
Spaniards.

Ribera goes on to tell how he convinced Mendoza to send help to
Juan de Ayolas and how he was ordered to go with Juan de Salazar
"to guide and advise him about the way and journey since I had

more experience." On the way back, Ribera writes, he agreed to the founding of a fort at Asunción and was later appointed *maestre mayor*, or first mate, of the fleet charged with moving the people up from Corpus Christi. Ribera also held the rank of *maestre mayor* under Governor Cabeza de Vaca, who sent him to explore a Paraguay River tributary. On this journey he encountered a Xarae leader who revealed the way to riches. Ribera, however, withheld some of the information he received:

> Before a certain notary named Juan de Valderas, who accompanied me when I explored the Yacareati River, I wrote some of what I learned in those natives' land—since I know and understand the Cario's language, I was able to communicate with them. I did not wish for the notary to know the substance of the report that they gave me; I wished to keep it secret and only reveal it to the governor. I was unable to inform him because of his illness and because subsequently he was imprisoned. Since this is the most important thing for the service of God and Your Majesty, I have kept it to myself until now and not told anyone in order to report to Your Majesty. I am sending the said written report as I heard it from the native *indios* of the said land so that Your Majesty may know the abundance that he possesses in this province.[37]

The ability to control the flow of information between the natives and the newcomers afforded interpreters such as Ribera an advantaged position in the ranks of the conquistadors. More important, these Spaniards' long-term immersion among the Guaraní allowed them to function as cultural mediators, able to communicate the expectations of both groups as they adjusted to coexistence. These transculturated castaways set the precedent for Spanish–Guaraní synergy in the Río de la Plata. The bilateral quality of the interaction is attested to by the fact that today both Guaraní and Spanish are official languages of Paraguay.

37. Ribera's *relación* appears at the end of Cabeza de Vaca's *Comentarios*, which were published in 1555. It describes, among other things, a nation of very small people, large towns rich in precious metals inhabited exclusively by women, beyond which lay cities of black men with pointed beards. Tuer (2011, 204) rightly sees in Ribera's account a combination of European fantasies with local perceptions of the Inca empire.

The Selected Letters

As a representative sample of a vast epistolary archive, the letters
contained in this volume tell the story of the early stages in the
conquest of the Río de la Plata, which started out as a highly doubt-
ful endeavor. At every turn, the first colonists faced risk. They found
themselves at the ends of the earth, far from both Europe and the
better-established colonial infrastructure in the Caribbean. For two
decades, what communication they had with Spain offered little
relief. They were plagued by constant hunger, hostile natives, and
internal strife. Within a year of arrival, overcome by sickness and
tribulation, the colony's first governor, Pedro de Mendoza, decided
to sail back to Spain, abandoning the colonists to their own uncer-
tain fate. Before leaving, he addressed a letter to his lieutenant, Juan
de Ayolas. The letter, included in this volume, attests to the anguish
caused by the seemingly insurmountable obstacles that the colony
faced. It also exposes the self-interested and sometimes underhanded
dealings involved in governing a colonial outpost that afflicted and
nearly wrecked the colonists' efforts.

The letters in this collection are organized by subject rather than
chronologically. Although Isabel de Guevara wrote her letter in 1556,
she paints a stark picture of the material conditions that the settlers
confronted in the early days of the colony. Contrary to the general
misperception that the conquest was carried out exclusively by men,
Guevara's letter reminds us of the important role played by Spanish women. When Mendoza's fleet reached the Río de la Plata, the
colonists found themselves in a scarce environment that forced them
to look to the natives to supplement their meager rations. Whenever
food could not be obtained through negotiation, the conquistadors
tried to take it by force. The first raid ordered by Mendoza provoked
the siege of Buenos Aires. In her letter, Guevara focuses on the
women's contributions during the colony's darkest hour, when it
was beset by hunger and warring natives. Guevara relates how, when
the men were incapacitated by starvation, sickness, and despair, the
women rallied to take on the role of providers, caretakers, and soldiers. Guevara's narrative is addressed to an imperial authority seeking recognition for her efforts and the proportionate reward to which
she felt entitled. The expectation that the reward would be relative
to the effort may have led to a certain degree of hyperbole added for

good measure—a common strategy. Nevertheless, it is certain that Spanish men and women had to contend with and overcome a dismal reality. The adverse circumstances led to some contentious decisions. At the center of each major controversy we find Domingo Martínez de Irala. His letter to Emperor Charles V traveled on the ship that was taking Álvar Núñez Cabeza de Vaca, the crown's appointed governor, back to Spain. According to this text, Irala had deposed and imprisoned Cabeza de Vaca in the name of justice. Irala's account also explains his controversial decision to abandon Buenos Aires and move all the colonists to Asunción for the sake of everyone's survival. Whether praised as commendable or decried as criminal, Irala's actions defined much of the first and most arduous stage in the colonization of the Río de la Plata.

Officers like Irala often needed to justify their deeds to the crown because practically any colonist could write the authorities to offer a particular version of events.[38] Francisco Galán's letter offers such an alternative account, disparaging the generally deficient leadership that he held responsible for the colony's many woes. At first glance, the critique may seem more reliable because the letter is not addressed to a court official nor does it request rewards. In contrast, Juan Pavón makes clear demands in his own critical account of Irala's actions. Addressing the *fiscal* of the Council of the Indies, which managed all matters related to Spain's transoceanic colonies, Pavón insists on justice for Irala's iniquitous misdeeds. From the outset, Pavón underscores that his addressee does not know him, immediately emphasizing that this should not interfere with the due process that he fully expects. His letter attests to his trust in the imperial bureaucracy and his faith in the power of written testimony. For these New World colonists, writing supported the impression that even in the farthest reaches of the empire they were not without legal recourse. Writing also strengthened the illusion of fairness in the context of a monarchy that aspired to absolute control over its domain.

The overt justification for Spain's conquest of the New World was spreading the Christian gospel. Therefore, every conquering expedition included one or more representatives of the Catholic Church who went along to minister to the crews and, perhaps more

---

38. Even illiterate colonists could dictate their missives to one of several notaries.

important, to convert the natives. The cleric Francisco de Andrada mentions the poor spiritual and moral condition of the colonists in Asunción, but he focuses primarily on his evangelical efforts among the local natives, highlighting his success. Andrada's letter paints a picture of a fertile field for the advancement of the Catholic faith, provided that his church be given sufficient material support and effective leadership. Thus, Andrada requests various cult items for the church and to be appointed bishop so that he may better tend to both his Spanish and Guaraní flocks.

The priests' mission often placed them at odds with the conquistadors, who were less concerned with the well-being—spiritual or otherwise—of the peoples they encountered in their search for riches. The cleric Martín González decries at length the systematic brutalities committed against the *indios* in the Río de la Plata, especially women. His narrative is replete with heart-wrenching and sometime gruesome images of the natives' plight: old women raking their breasts to feed babies whose mothers had been kidnapped, unattended children walking aimlessly into open fires, and whole villages deserted to escape the insatiable lust of the Spaniards. González's stance as a defender of the *indios* likely prompted him to exaggerate on occasion, but his letter paints a vivid picture of an undeniably violent climate.

Amid the harsh realities of conquest, the colonists had to tend to their everyday needs. Scarcity forced them to adapt and to innovate. Domingo Martínez was neither soldier nor cleric, but rather an eager young man seeking to make his fortune in the New World. He neither fought nor preached. Instead, he taught himself a trade that allowed him to supply items that would make life more comfortable: knives, fishhooks, needles, and combs. Martínez boasts of rendering many practical and profitable services, which included designing gadgets and machines to increase the colony's productivity. In describing his entrepreneurial pursuits, Martínez provides revealing information about the colony's rapport with the indentured natives. His letter portrays the *indios* as conniving beasts who must be policed closely to prevent them from cheating their Spanish masters. However, the depiction reveals the working relationship between the two groups: the colony's prosperity depended heavily on the labor of natives, who were far from passive. The intimate rapport between the Spanish and the Guaraní led to a growing *mestizo* population, which Martínez viewed as a threat, his numerous *mestiza* daughters notwithstanding. This letter captures exceptionally well the paradoxes that result from the fraught interactions between the colonizers and the colonized.

PROVENANCE AND PUBLICATION HISTORY

The manuscripts of most of the letters written from the Río de la Plata are housed in the Archivo General de Indias in Seville among thousands of legal documents related to its contested governance. Several letters were published in the late nineteenth and early twentieth century as uncommented appendices in sundry historiographic volumes. A set of letters kept at the Archivo Histórico Nacional in Madrid, all of which are dated in 1556, appeared in the collection of *Cartas de Indias,* published by the Spanish Ministerio de Fomento in 1877.[39] Many documents related to the early colonial period, including some of the early letters, were expertly transcribed for the five volumes of the *Documentos históricos y geográficos relativos a la conquista y colonización rioplatense,* which were published in 1941 by the official commission for the four hundredth anniversary of the first founding of Buenos Aires.

The early letters from the Río de la Plata are valuable primary sources for envisioning the complexities of the conquest and colonization processes. However, those that have been published are dispersed in old and rare volumes. Further, to our knowledge, only two of the letters have been translated into English.[40] The letters chosen for this collection offer an English-speaking audience a representative sample of the many stories behind the Río de la Plata's conquest and colonization.

---

39. The collection was reprinted in the Biblioteca de Autores Españoles in 1974; the publisher Porrúa produced a facsimile of the earlier edition in 2008. Digital images of this set of letters are available online through the Portal de Archivos Españoles (http://pares.mcu.es/).

40. Two letters from 1556, including the one written by Isabel de Guevara, were translated and included in *Letters and People of the Spanish Indies: Sixteenth Century,* a wide-ranging anthology edited by James Lockhart and Enrique Otte (1976). As it is one of the very rare testimonies by women who participated in the front lines of the Spanish conquest, Guevara's text has been included in volumes that do not deal directly with the conquest of the Río de la Plata, such as Nina Scott's work on early Spanish American women writers (1999).

THIS TRANSLATION

Any act of translation involves choices. The letters collected here present particular challenges resulting from the language, the style, and the circumstances in which they were composed. Many words refer to titles, offices, institutions, and practices specific to the Spanish bureaucracy of the period. These and other Spanish words that have no direct equivalent in English appear italicized in the text and are explained in the glossary at the end of the volume. We have also decided not to translate the masculine *indio(s)* and the feminine *india(s)*. Beyond the mistaken geographic reference, these words have pejorative connotations that terms such as "Indian" or "native" do not convey accurately.

The reader should also keep in mind that these letters were composed by the flight of the pen, so to speak. The writing was hampered by the lack of paper, which did not allow for drafting and correcting. For the same reason, narratives can seem convoluted when, for instance, the author makes chronological leaps to add a piece of information or an explanation previously omitted. Moreover, it is easy to lose track of the many spatial and temporal cross-references, many of which take for granted the addressee's background knowledge. Our translation attempts to offer the modern English-speaking reader a clear narrative while preserving the flavor of the original sixteenth-century Spanish. The notes provide contextual information, clarification as needed, and references to useful secondary sources.

Selected Letters from the Río de la Plata

Pedro de Mendoza to Juan de Ayolas (April 21, 1537)

As Governor Pedro de Mendoza prepared to set sail for Spain, he made
sure to leave clear instructions regarding how the enterprise that had
cost him so dearly should be managed in his absence.[1] In keeping
with the notarial culture of Hapsburg Spain, he made sure to have a
copy of the document made: it might be needed as evidence in a legal
process—as indeed it was.

The most striking feature of Mendoza's letter to Juan de Ayolas is
its candor. Somewhat rambling at times, the text conveys the regrets
and the hopes of a dying man. This letter also sheds light on the
entrepreneurial side of the conquest by showing that many conquistadors were also businessmen, and partners as much as vassals of the
Spanish crown. Thus, for instance, the would-be-governors negoti-
ated *capitulaciones*, or contracts that specified mutual obligations.
Mendoza promised, for example, to make two trips to the Río de la
Plata, each time taking five hundred men, one hundred horses, and
a year's worth of supplies at his expense. Among other things, the
crown accorded Mendoza a twelfth part of the royal fifth (net after
expenditures, not gross), exempted him from paying taxes on any
personal property taken to the Río de la Plata for six years (unless
he sold or traded it), and gave him the right to appoint an heir who
would be allowed to fulfill and benefit from the terms of the contract
in case of Mendoza's untimely death. Once obtained from the king,
grants and titles could be bought and sold—though the deal would
always require royal ratification.

As in any business, resources had to be managed. Mendoza reveals
that human resources posed the greatest challenge and offers honest

1. Archivo General de Indias, Papeles antiguos de buen gobierno: Perú, patronato,
185, R.12.

advice on how to deal with individuals whose ambition matched the riches that they hoped to find in the Río de la Plata. At times it seems that the only thing keeping conquistador society from self-destruction was a concerted adherence to judicial procedures. Even so, as Mendoza points out, there were special cases in which these were best sidestepped, albeit discreetly. Or else, formal legal proceedings could be undertaken after the sentence had been carried out. This is what happened in the case of Juan Osorio, who was secretly charged with and found guilty of plotting mutiny; the public inquiry was conducted after his execution.

Mendoza's missive never reached Ayolas, who died pursuing the land's fabled riches. As a result, the rights to the governorship of the Río de la Plata would be contested both on-site and in the courts of Spain for over a decade.

———◆●◆———

This is a copy of the instructions that Don Pedro de Mendoza, deceased, left for Juan de Ayolas, his lieutenant governor, at the time when the said Don Pedro set sail for Spain; it was found in the desk of the said Don Pedro at the time when his goods from the ship were inventoried; and it is as follows:

This is what my lieutenant governor, Juan de Ayolas, must do if it pleases God that he return; and if he were not to return, [what] Captain Salazar [must do].

Take all the people from upriver and, from here, all those who can fit in the brigantines. And if he were able to find a different way, set fire to those ships or sink them, and take all the people [farther] upriver. This I leave to his discretion because if those who are here are able to work and sow, they will be able to endure. And to stay with the ships, thirty men will suffice. And anyway, as I said, I leave this to the discretion of the said Juan de Ayolas. And if he should think best to take all the people, let him take the barge on which he can carry them all. And if he cannot go beyond Sancti Spíritus[2] with the barge, leave it there and take those who can sail on the brigantines, and return to the barge by a different route so that all the people can be together wherever the said Juan de Ayolas finds a

---

2. The fort established near the Paraná River by Sebastian Cabot in 1527 and razed by natives in 1529.

suitable location. And if he should decide to go directly to the other sea,[3] let him do so. But let him always leave a settlement on the Paraguay River or somewhere else he sees fit so that we may always know where he is and so that the people that I send to him may find him. And insofar as I grant him authority to remove captains and name others, it is my will that he not remove without cause those that I have named so far. And if his lieutenants or second lieutenants should give him cause, let him remove and punish them. But let him not remove the companies from the captains but rather place different lieutenants or second lieutenants instead of the said captains that I have named.

You are to be wary of the individuals of whom you know I was wary. And those that I trusted I well think you may trust.

Take on all of my servants and employ them, because they are good and trustworthy, especially Ortega,[4] who is staying behind. Accept him as a servant immediately.

If Salazar[5] should want to go to Spain to be my steward, send him along with Captain Francisco Ruiz.[6] For now Ruiz is to remain here so that, if it please God, he may bring me news of what you have done, as well as some pearl or jewel that you may have gotten for me because you know that, unless I sell my properties, I do not even have food to eat in Spain. I place all my hope in God and in you. Therefore, see that you not forget me, since you are like a son to me and I am leaving you with such a worthy charge, and because I leave with six or seven wounds, four of them on my head, and one on my leg, and another on my hand that does not let me write or even sign my name.

Treat Captain Francisco Ruiz well, because I love him dearly. He is from the same region as I, and you know that we grew up together.

3. The Pacific Ocean, also known as Mar del Sur.

4. Those in command charged Juan de Ortega with several tasks after Mendoza's departure, the most significant of which was a failed attempt to dismantle the settlement at Buenos Aires in July 1540. Domingo de Irala personally took care of this task one year later.

5. Juan de Salazar de Espinosa, the founder of Asunción. In 1545, Álvar Núñez Cabeza de Vaca appointed him governor in his stead. However, he was arrested by the rebels shortly thereafter and sent to Spain with Cabeza de Vaca. He later returned to the Río de la Plata to serve as *tesorero*.

6. Francisco Ruiz Galán. Mendoza appointed Ruiz Galán as lieutenant governor in Buenos Aires, which led to an extended conflict with Irala.

Send him quickly because, if it please God that he bring the means, I will send him back quickly with people and brigantines so that he may go up the river without stopping.

And if those who stayed with me, who are Antonio de Mendoza and Antonio de Angulo, should serve you well, honor them. And if not, do not worry about them. Let everyone know that they must carry their own weight in service.

If you should put anyone on trial, let it be with great reason. And if it were for something you could let pass, do so, because this will serve God. If it is not, do not execute him without due process first and without solid proof. If the case were treason against you, and this you truly found to be true, and should you not find enough witnesses, push him into a well, secretly, by night, or throw him some place where he will not be found and cannot harm you. But first, as I have told you, remember God, for though you are young, you are shrewd, so do all things in God. I leave you the commands and decrees from the king. Keep them safe so that you may make use of them.

I am leaving certain parcels of land allotted to the king's officials and to Francisco Ruiz, who goes with me, and to my servants, and to the sailors. Should God give us any wealth, once my expenses have been covered, it is right that Captain Francisco Ruiz and the king's officials should have some profit as well.

I am taking the *contador*[7] so as not to leave such a seditious man here and also because he would have stayed grudgingly. His brother is staying as his lieutenant; treat him well, and praise his brother to him. Make yourself well loved by the honest men whom you find trustworthy.

Should you enter so far inland that you run into Almagro or Pizarro,[8] try to befriend them. And if you are strong enough to do it, do not let anyone trespass on your claim. And if you are not, at least

---

7. Juan de Cáceres, brother of Felipe de Cáceres, who stayed behind and took over the office of *contador*.

8. After overpowering the Inca in Cusco, Francisco Pizarro (1478–1541) became governor of Nueva Castilla in 1534. Diego de Almagro (1475–1538), who had participated in the conquest of Peru alongside Pizarro, was appointed governor of Nueva Toledo, a large swath of land that bordered Pizarro's governorship in the north and Mendoza's in the south. In 1537, after an unfruitful expedition to the south, Almagro returned to Peru in order to take over Cuzco, alleging that it fell within his jurisdiction. In 1538, Pizarro defeated Almagro's forces and had him executed.

perform your *requerimientos*[9] and always try to keep them as friends but without allowing your people to go over to them.

And if Diego de Almagro should want to give you 150,000 ducats[10] (as he gave Pedro de Alvarado to return to his own territory)[11] so that I relinquish my governorship of that coast and those islands, and even if it is just 100,000, do it, unless you see that something else would be more profitable to me, not letting me die of hunger. And should you do it, by this document signed with my name, I promise to comply with all that you decide and to accept it, and to make sure that the king validates it. And it must be on the condition that [Almagro] leaves you at the port with one of his servants, and that you carry the money, and he must leave you at the port of Panama.[12] And so that we may abide by each other, I promise to give you 8,000 ducats, or a tenth of whatever price you can get for it. And if God should give you some jewel or stone, make sure to send it to me so that I may have some remedy for my travails and my sores. I do not send you written authorization, so as not to reveal this to anyone, except for this document on which I have signed my name.

I paid Tovalina fifty ducats out of the ninety that he says you owe him, and I took a receipt. I say this so that you do not have to pay them to him again.

And though above I say that the deal that you should make with Almagro or Pizarro should be for the two hundred leagues that I have as governor in the Mar del Sur or the islands, I say that you do it for all of the Río de la Plata as well, and for as much as you can manage.

Francisco Ruiz will give you the remaining belongings of the deceased, as well as certain valuables that belong to me, and those of

---

9. Mendoza is probably not referring to the infamous *requerimiento* that was to be read aloud to the natives of the New World requiring them to submit peacefully or be conquered without mercy, but to the formalities required for claiming territorial rights.

10. The relative value of such a sum may be gauged against the cost of Mendoza's well-funded expedition, which according to Enrique de Gandía (1936a, 94) was 12,000 ducats.

11. Pedro de Alvarado (1485–1541) participated in the conquest of Mexico and led the conquest of Guatemala. In 1535, he undertook the exploration of the region north of Peru. Diego de Almagro paid Alvarado 100,000 gold pesos to relinquish his fleet and to desist from the enterprise (López de Gómara 1979, 188).

12. This stipulation guaranteed that Ayolas would be able to return to Spain in a timely manner owing to the regular communication between Spain and Peru through the Isthmus of Panama.

Alemán. Name Juan Ramos and Martín Pérez storekeepers, and order them to safeguard the stores better than has been done until now, because everything was lost.

I would very much like to speak to you before leaving, but my ailment and time do not permit me to wait any longer than I have.

Act so that you may be governor for life, remembering first God and then me, because if you should not do so, I will send another governor.

Here I leave you two sealed testaments: one that I made and another that I have amended. And a copy of the amended one remains with the notary. And if God should see fit to take me, you may open them and see what they contain. And in everything else, I defer to your sound judgment. Written in the port of our Lady of Buenos Aires on the twenty-first of April in the year 1537.

P.S. If God should see fit that you find some gold or silver, you will deduct the costs I have incurred, which you have in writing, and you will set aside for me 16 percent, for you 8 percent, 4 for the captains, and for the rest [to each] according to their service. And set in writing before a notary what you give to each one. I cannot find in the desk the ledger of what you have spent. For my sake, send it with Captain Francisco Ruiz, along with any promissory notes that you may have, because I am missing many documents. Written as above.

------◆◆◆------

Isabel Guevara to Princess Juana (July 2, 1556)

Women were present at every stage of the conquest of the New World. Thirty women sailed on Christopher Columbus's third transatlantic journey. Juan Francisco Maura (2005, 185–91) calls attention to the women who participated in the conquest of Mexico by nursing the wounded, keeping the watch, encouraging the men, and taking up arms alongside them. Richard Konetzke (1945, 124) contends that except for a few special cases, the Spanish government never sought to prevent women from traveling to the New World. On the contrary, measures were enacted to promote the migration of women because the crown understood that the security and stability of its possessions across the sea depended on establishing an enduring Spanish presence. Konetzke (1945, 146) estimates that women accounted for 10 percent of the total number of Spaniards who journeyed to America between 1509 and 1538. According to Kamen (2003, 243), the number had increased to one-sixth of all licensed travelers by the 1550s, and to a third by the 1560s.

Isabel de Guevara was just one of many women who participated in Pedro de Mendoza's expedition. The names of several of them are preserved in the partial roster of the people who sailed with Mendoza, as well as in legal documents. They include Ana de Arrieta, María Dávila, Elvira Gutierres, Leonor Gutierres, Catalina Pérez, Elvira Pineda, Mari Sánchez, and Catalina de Vadillo (Gandía 1936a, 96). However, Guevara is unique among them for having written about her experience.[13] Her letter vividly describes the crucial role that women played during the first and most difficult year of life in Buenos Aires. The settlers were under constant threat from the natives and beleaguered by such hunger that some allegedly ate from the bodies of the dead—understandably, this document does not broach that ghastly matter. Guevara details all the things the women did to ensure the group's survival, taking care not to discredit the men by attributing their poor performance to sickness and lack of nourishment. Her treatment of the delicate subject of male honor provides rare insight into the gender dynamic in these early settlements.

Guevara's letter also illustrates the most recurrent complaint in the letters written in 1556. Many colonists were dissatisfied with their allotment of *indios encomendados*, which, they felt, was not proportionate to their exertions in the conquest of the land or sufficient to maintain an appropriate living standard. Indigenous labor was the only significant source of wealth in the province, so anyone without an *encomienda* was condemned to work hard for a paltry living. Domingo de Irala is said to have distributed 20,000 natives among 320 conquistadors, giving his supporters more than a fair share. An equal allocation would probably have caused as much protest since every *encomendero* or *encomendera* would only have received 62 or 63 *indios*. Even the larger *encomiendas* in the Río de la Plata were minuscule compared to those in more populous parts of the New World.

13. Archivo Histórico Nacional, Colección Documentos de Indias, diversoscolecciones, 24, N.18.

The conquistadors who were inclined to voice their disappointment to the king generally highlighted their extraordinary efforts in the service of the empire. Guevara's willingness to go above and beyond the call of duty to ensure the subsistence of the budding colony ostensibly merits the *encomienda* she wishes for herself. The request highlights the peripheral position of the province because by the mid-sixteenth century, the crown's policies and the decline of the indigenous population had significantly undermined the viability of *encomiendas* in all but outlying regions like the Río de la Plata (McCreery 2000, 33–34). There, *encomiendas* were first established in 1556, and long after that its governors still had the right to grant them—and even regrant them—for three generations (Service 1951, 243). Local conditions generated other departures from standard practices. For instance, *encomenderos* could legally collect tribute from their allotted *indios*, but were forbidden by law from demanding labor without compensation.[14] However, as Elman Service (1951, 136) points out, that stipulation was systematically disregarded in the Río de la Plata because the economic conditions were such that labor was the only tribute to be had. Moreover, labor obligations were integral to the Guaraní social economy long before the Spaniards learned to exploit them. As in several contemporaneous letters, Guevara asks that her *encomienda* be awarded in perpetuity. The duration of *encomiendas* had long been debated, but the crown had consistently resisted perpetual grants.[15]

After asking for her everlasting *encomienda*, Guevara goes even further in her letter by requesting a position for her husband, Pedro

14. Rules for *encomiendas* were issued on several occasions, always aiming to curtail the practice. The most serious threat to system came in 1542, when the New Laws governing the treatment of the natives were issued. However, they were strongly resisted in the colonies and were not fully implemented.

15. One of the more influential voices in the debate was that of Bartolomé de las Casas (1484–1566), whose ongoing advocacy for indigenous rights elicited much of the legislation against *encomiendas*. On the crown's legislative efforts in favor of the *indios* see Hanke (1949); on their inefficacy, see Keen (1969). As late as 1554, the *encomenderos* of Peru offered King Philip II a large sum of money for the concession in perpetuity of their *encomiendas* and full judicial rights over their allotted natives. After years of consultation and discussion, in 1562 the Council of the Indies convinced the king to refuse any such privileges. The need to preserve royal authority in the New World was one of the decisive arguments; another was the crown's duty to safeguard the natives (Brading 1993, 70–71).

de Esquivel. Esquivel had arrived to the Río de la Plata along with Álvar Núñez Cabeza de Vaca. When the second *adelantado* was deposed, Esquivel supported Juan de Salazar's bid for lieutenant governor. He later had to be forced to join the *entrada* led by Irala in 1547. In other words, Esquivel was one of the *leales* who opposed Irala's governorship. Guevara blames her husband's loyalties for the injustice done against her despite being one of the *conquistadores viejos*, those who had arrived with Pedro de Mendoza in 1536. Along with her strong character, her seniority may have been one of the factors that allowed Guevara to save Esquivel's life on the three occasions it was threatened by Irala and his supporters, as her words imply.[16]

Guevara's letter is also exceptional for being addressed to Juana de Austria, the daughter of Charles V, who at the time was serving as regent of Spain. Juana remained in charge of the kingdom from 1554 to 1559 in the absence of her father, who was fighting the French, and her brother Phillip, who was away in England and later in Flanders.[17] Like Isabel de Guevara, Princess Juana broke gender barriers as the only female Jesuit. In 1554 she secretly took vows in the Jesuit order under the name Mateo Sánchez and devoted herself to a monastic lifestyle until her death in 1573. According to Rosa Helena Chinchilla (2004, 21), Princess Juana greatly influenced the courtly literary tastes and devotional ideals that became famous under her brother, King Philip II. Perhaps Guevara thought it improper for a woman to address the king directly. She may have also reckoned that a woman would be more responsive to her request than a man, whether it was the king or any of the members of the Council of the Indies. In any case, Guevara rightly addresses her letter to the highest authority in Spain at the time.

———————

16. One of Irala's followers did eventually succeed in killing Guevara's husband. According to data provided by Lafuente (1943, 210), Esquivel was arrested and executed for treason in 1571 by Felipe de Cáceres, who was lieutenant governor at the time (see the epilogue). The date of Guevara's death is unknown.

17. Started in 1551 by Henry II of France, the Hapsburg–Valois War lasted until the Spanish defeated the French in 1559. In 1554, Philip left for England to marry Queen Mary. A year later, he was in the Netherlands to take over the Flemish throne abdicated by his father. In 1556, Charles also abdicated the Spanish throne in favor of his son. However, King Philip II did not return to Spain until 1559.

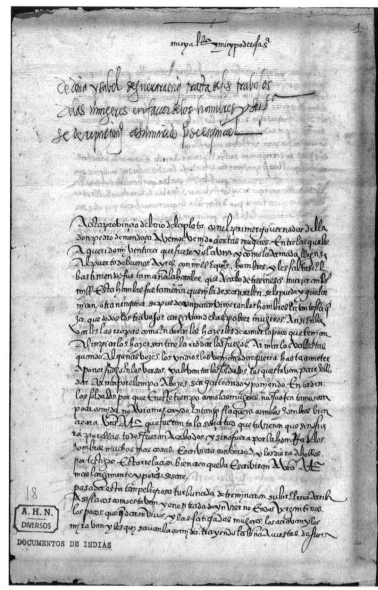

FIG. 1 Manuscript of Isabel de Guevara's letter, fol. 1r. España, Ministerio de Educación, Cultura y Deporte. Archivo Histórico Nacional. Diversos-Colecciones, 24, N.18.

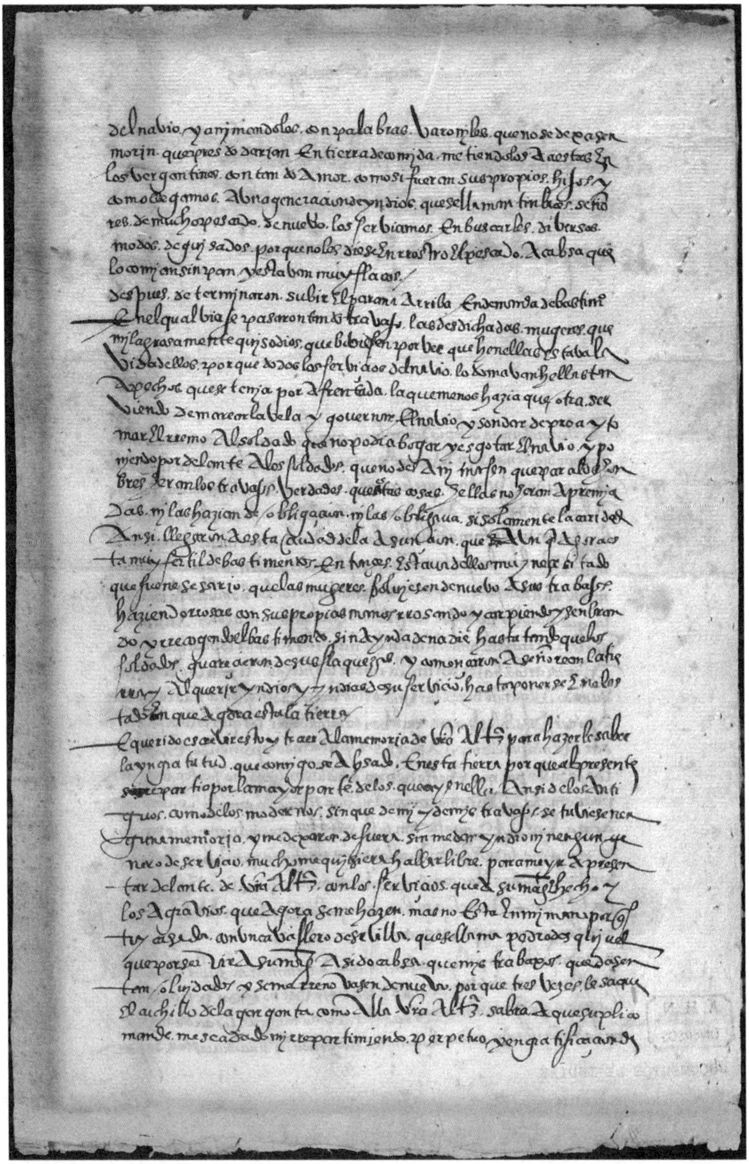

FIG. 2 Manuscript of Isabel de Guevara's letter, fol. 1v. España, Ministerio de Educación, Cultura y Deporte. Archivo Histórico Nacional. Diversos-Colecciones, 24, N.18.

FIG. 3 Manuscript of Isabel de Guevara's letter, fol. 2r. España, Ministerio de Educación, Cultura y Deporte. Archivo Histórico Nacional. Diversos-Colecciones, 24, N.18.

Most High and Powerful Lady,

It was my fate to be one of a number of women who came to this province of Río de la Plata with its first governor, Don Pedro de Mendoza. After the fleet arrived at the port of Buenos Aires with fifteen hundred men, when their provisions ran out, hunger was such that by the end of three months one thousand had died. So great was this hunger that no other, not even Jerusalem's,[18] compares. The men came to be so weak that the poor women took charge of all the chores, everything from washing their clothes to taking care of them, preparing what little food they had, washing them, keeping the watch, and stoking the fires. Whenever the *indios* came to make war, we loaded the crossbows, ignited the fuses on the guns, roused the able-bodied soldiers, raised the alarm throughout the camp, and assembled and commanded the troops. Because at this time, since we women live on less food, we had not become as weak as the men. Your Highness can be certain that the attentiveness of the women was such that if not for them, it would have been over for us all. And if it were not for the men's reputation, I would faithfully tell many more things and make them bear witness. I do believe that these events will be related to Your Highness more extensively, and so I will stop here.

Once we overcame this dangerous tribulation, the few people who were still alive decided to go upriver[19]—weak as they were and with winter setting in—in two brigantines. The exhausted women took care of them, watched over them, and cooked their food. The women hauled firewood to the boat; they encouraged the men with manly words, telling them not to give up and die, that soon they would come to a place with food; and they carried them onto the brigantines with as much love as if they were their children. We came upon the Timbues, an indigenous people who had fish aplenty. And once again we served the men by finding new ways of cooking the fish so they would not get sick of it, given that they ate it without bread and were so weak.

18. Possibly a reference to the biblical seven-year famine that, according to the Book of Genesis, took place during the time of Jacob (Gen. 41).

19. This could be Pedro de Mendoza's 1536 journey from Buenos Aires to Corpus Christi, the fort founded by Juan de Ayolas.

Afterward, they determined to go up the Paraná in search of food. During the journey, the wretched women had so many travails that it was a miracle that God, seeing that the men's lives depended on the women, allowed them to live. The women took all the ship's tasks so much to heart that anyone who did less than another felt ashamed. They trimmed the sails, they steered the ship, they sounded at the bow, and took the oar from the soldier who could not row or bail water. They put the men first so they would not get discouraged, since these were men's tasks. In truth, the women were not compelled, nor did they do these tasks out of duty; charity alone obliged them. Thus, they came to the city of Asunción.[20] Though the city is now rich in provisions, then it was in such dire need that it was necessary for the women to return to their toils. They stubbed with their bare hands, clearing and weeding the fields, reaping and sowing the harvests, without anyone's help, until the soldiers recovered from their weakness and began to lord over the land, taking *indios* and *indias* into their service, until the land came to be as it is today.

I wanted to write this and bring it to the attention of Your Highness in order to inform you of the ungratefulness that I have been subject to in this land. By now most of the people here, both the veterans and the newcomers, have received their cut, without any regard for me or for my hardships; they left me out, without giving me a single *indio* or any kind of service. I wish I had the freedom to go and present myself before Your Highness, to recount the services that I have rendered His Majesty and the wrongs I am now being done. Alas, it is not in my power because I am married to a gentleman from Seville, called Pedro d'Esquivel,[21] who, because of his service to His Majesty, has caused my labors to be forgotten and even renewed, since, as Your Highness will have heard, three times I saved his neck from the knife's edge. In view of this, I beg you to order that I be given my *repartimiento* in perpetuity, and as a reward for my services that my husband be given a position worthy of his caliber; for his own part, owing to his service, he deserves it. May Our Lord

---

20. The journey must have taken place in the fall of 1537. In fact, Asunción only became a city when its *cabildo*, or council, was instituted in 1541.

21. The fact that Pedro de Esquivel was part of the crew that traveled to the Río de la Plata in Álvar Núñez Cabeza de Vaca's fleet may explain why he and his wife were slighted in Irala's *repartimiento* (Scott 1999, 6).

increase your royal life and estate for many a long year. From this city of Asunción, July 2, 1556.

Your Highness's servant who kisses your royal hands,
Doña Isabel de Guevara.

Domingo de Irala to Emperor Charles V (March 1, 1545)

Though Governor Pedro de Mendoza's instructions attempted to account for any number of circumstances that could arise in his absence, he left no instructions regarding the governance of the colony should his lieutenant, Juan de Ayolas, fail to come back from his *entrada*. When Ayolas did not return, his lieutenant, Domingo de Irala, had to dispute his claim to the governorship with Francisco Ruiz Galán, who was left in charge of Buenos Aires by Mendoza with the proviso that he would be under the authority of Ayolas upon his return. Later, Irala vied for power with Álvar Núñez Cabeza de Vaca, eventually deposing him. Given that Cabeza de Vaca's authority came directly from the crown, this was a brazen move that could easily be considered seditious. As such, it had to be thoughtfully explained.

Irala's letter to the emperor depicts his actions since Mendoza's departure in 1537 as substantial contributions to the success of the colony and, therefore, as valuable service to the crown.[22] Irala paints himself as Ayolas's faithful subordinate who meticulously prepares for all scenarios, seeing to it that the land is pacified and the settlements remain well supplied. The letter is as remarkable for what it says as for what it omits: Irala glosses over his drawn-out conflicts with Ruiz Galán, neglects to mention that the decision to dismantle Buenos Aires was highly controversial among officers and settlers, and exculpates himself for the contentious arrest of Cabeza de Vaca, a royal appointee being sent as a prisoner back to Spain.

The myriad factual details included in the letter belie Irala's artful manipulation of his account to put a positive spin on every deed, even those that could be the subject of controversy. He acts as though he were grateful for the assistance that Cabeza de Vaca's arrival

---

22. Archivo General de Indias, justicia. Autos fiscales. Charcas. Justicia, 1131.

represented rather than feeling threatened by a prospective rival. Irala notes that as long as Cabeza de Vaca was recognized as governor, he dutifully followed the chain of command and obeyed orders even when it meant carrying out mercenary duties. He takes credit, nonetheless, for all that was done to keep the land at peace and the settlements supplied. Irala claims that it was only when the people decided to arrest Cabeza de Vaca and elected him instead that he began to act as governor. Thereafter, all of Irala's decisions appear to contribute to the survival of the colony and the creation of suitable conditions to continue the search for precious metal, rather than to the pursuit of a personal quest for power. This report conveniently downplays his role in Cabeza de Vaca's imprisonment and overlooks the ensuing controversies, which lasted for more than a year.

Irala's letter is replete with irony. In order to justify what appears as dereliction of duty and abuse of power, the narrative underscores his loyalty at every turn. For instance, Irala keeps going out to look for Juan de Ayolas, stopping only when his boats become so tattered that they sink. Likewise, Irala claims to have remained faithful to Cabeza de Vaca right up until his arrest. Other ironies may seem humorous today but highlight important issues. For example, Irala sarcastically describes an attack he suffered as an example of the natives' "customary friendship" with the Spaniards, but in other moments we are reminded that the Spaniards' very survival did, in fact, depend on friendly natives bringing them provisions and acting as allies against other native groups. The account here also illustrates the paradoxes of the conquistadors' documentary culture. Irala's attention to minutiae often borders on the absurd. While the particulars of his account might serve to establish veracity, he is quite forthcoming about his use of the written word to deceive other conquistadors who might find the abandoned settlement of Buenos Aires. Irala openly acknowledges his attempt to use language as a performative speech act to shape reality to his will.

Finally, by emphasizing Irala's incessant activity, the letter indicates the seemingly insurmountable challenges that these conquistadors faced. They were forced to go up and down the rivers continually, traveling in cycles, their range limited by the amount of provisions they could carry or find along the way and by the durability of their ships. Likewise, the chain of command was frequently threatened by ambition or by circumstance. Yet even as the community teetered on the edge chaos, the semblance of due process that was maintained through writing afforded the colonists of the Río de la Plata a measure of order. Ultimately, what allowed them to survive and, eventually, to thrive against all odds was their resourcefulness and the unwavering resoluteness manifested in their texts.

———•◆•———

Holy, Cesarean, Catholic Majesty,

On the fourteenth day of October of 1536, Don Pedro de Mendoza, who was governor of this province, sent his lieutenant Juan de Ayolas from the port of Buena Esperanza with two brigantines and a caravel, as well as one hundred seventy men, to explore this river and to see with his own eyes where there might be some precious metals or mines. Following orders as diligently as he could, and despite great obstacles (such as the loss of the caravel and the capsizing of a brigantine in a storm), he arrived at the port of La Candelaria, which is on the Paraguay River (at nineteen and two-thirds degrees), where he found a nation of *indios* called Payagoas. He found among them a former slave of a certain García,[23] a Christian[24] who took some precious metal to the island of Santa Catalina. The slave offered to guide Ayolas to where the said García had acquired the said metal. With this information, he decided to follow the road indicated by the slave; so that he might do it better, the chief of the Payagoas gave him thirty *indios* as porters. And so he left with one hundred thirty men on the twelfth of February of 1537, leaving me in his stead with the two brigantines and thirty-three men. He ordered all who remained to obey me in the name of Your Majesty and of the said governor. I was to wait for him as long as I could sustain myself in the brigantines, and for that purpose he left me six or seven measures of corn; everything else I was to get from the Payagoa chief, whom he left as my friend.

With much effort, I supported myself with fish from the *indios*, going up and down the river, until the twenty-third of June of the said year when, by order of the governor, Captain Juan de Salazar de Espinoza[25] came with two brigantines looking for Juan de Ayolas.

---

23. Alejo García, the shipwreck from the 1516 Juan de Solís expedition.
24. In early-modern Spanish texts, Christian always means Catholic.
25. See note 5 in Pedro de Mendoza's letter.

When the *indios* saw him coming, they were so disturbed that they fled. Lacking provisions and because my ships were in such a state that I could barely keep them afloat, we agreed that I should retreat to this [Cario–Guaraní] nation, both to restock the supplies and to repair the ships so that I could return to the said port. And so it was done. And because it was advantageous to Your Majesty's service and to the pacification and settlement of this land, we made a house at this port,[26] where we reside at present (which is thirty-five and a half degrees, in the land of the Guaraní), so that it might serve as our refuge and as lodging for those who come from downriver. This was done with all diligence.

Once it was done, Captain Juan de Salazar left to report to the governor this state of affairs, leaving a certain Gonzalo de Mendoza[27] as captain of the said fortress. Having acquired some supplies, I returned to the port of La Candelaria to wait for news of the said Juan de Ayolas. There, I heard from the Payagoas, and after twelve days, they hid from me again. And because I was running out of supplies and the ships were sinking for having been poorly repaired due to lack of materials, and also because they told me that Juan de Ayolas was very far from the river, I came down to this port where my ships sank on arrival, for they could no longer float. And so it happened that a few days later, Francisco Ruiz Galán,[28] whom the said governor had left as his lieutenant at the port of Buenos Aires with the people there, arrived in Asunción. Seeing the great need of supplies in the land (due to the locusts that destroyed everything), he had to return downriver, leaving Captain Juan de Salazar with fifty men at this port. Ruíz Galán gave me a brigantine so that I could go to the port of La Candelaria to get news of Juan de Ayolas. Having gathered some supplies, I went up to the port of La Candelaria and arrived on the twenty-third of August of the year 1538. There, the Payagoas came to me and, in keeping with our customary friendship, they killed four

26. Asunción.
27. Gonzalo de Mendoza had accompanied Salazar de Espinoza in his search for Ayolas and in his founding of Asunción. Later, he would also play a consequential role by finding and leading Alonso Cabrera's ship from Santa Catalina Island to Buenos Aires.
28. See note 6 in Pedro de Mendoza's letter. Here Irala conveniently omits the drawn-out dispute over who was the legitimate leader in Pedro de Mendoza's and Juan de Ayolas's absence: Ruiz Galán, by direct word of Pedro de Mendoza, or Irala as stand-in for Ayolas; the dispute would be renewed in 1539.

of my men and wounded me and the rest of the people, so I had to come down to Asunción to look for food.

Captain Salazar and I were here on June 19 of the year 1539, when Francisco Ruiz Galán and the *veedor* Alonso Cabrera came with a decree from Your Majesty, ordering Cabrera to obey and to support the person or persons named therein. The said decree and the power left by the said governor Don Pedro de Mendoza referred specifically to Juan de Ayolas and, in his absence, to me. So, in accordance with my own authority and mandate, I summoned them. After seeing and examining the said documents, the said Alonso Cabrera obeyed me and offered to give me all the help and support ordered by Your Majesty. And all the people and the captains did likewise.

Seeing that Governor Juan de Ayolas was in need of help, I gathered supplies and other necessary things for the journey and, with two hundred eighty men, went upriver in search of him. I arrived at the port of La Candelaria on the sixteenth of January of the year 1540. On the way, I was informed by these Cario *indios* that some of the Christians who had gone with Governor Juan de Ayolas had returned. In order to verify this, I left three brigantines with eighty men in the port of San Sebastián (which is eight leagues south of La Candelaria) while I prepared everything we needed for the journey. Then, I went with the rest of the crew in search of the Payagoas to find out about this with as much certainty as possible.

The Payagoas had apparently fled, because I could not find them in the places where they usually were. It pleased Our Lord that we captured a canoe with six Payagoas, one of whom had gone with Governor Juan de Ayolas. They said the governor was alive with most of the people and that he had built a fort in a nation of *indios* called Mayas [Mbaya]. They told of how he had sent back some Christians with some precious metal; this *indio* had come with them. The said Payagoas had killed ten or twelve Christians while they were in their houses.

Attending to our priorities, I proceeded with all diligence and brevity so that I would not run out of supplies while looking for these Payagoas. And so, leaving a certain Juan de Ortega[29] in the said San Sebastián with the brigantines and seventy men, on the fourteenth of February of the said year 1540, I left with the rest of the

29. See note 4 in Pedro de Mendoza's letter.

crew to succor the said governor, taking the said Payagoas as guides. In that year, God saw fit to send so much rain that, because the earth is so low and desolate, huge swamps developed. In the eighteen days that we walked through them, the water was never below our waists. And some days we could not even find a place to build a campfire for cooking. After eighteen days, seeing the men's weakness and the fact that the swamps kept growing and the supplies were lacking, in agreement with the clerics, the captains, and Your Majesty's officials, I turned back. We returned to the port of San Sebastián.

While I was preparing to come back down to Asunción to restock, a fifteen- or sixteen-year-old youth came to the brigantines. He said he came from inland, from a nation called Chane. He said that Governor Juan de Ayolas had returned to the port of La Candelaria with all the remaining people, and that the Payagoas, seeing that they were ill, tired, and without munitions (neither gunpowder nor crossbow strings), dared to kill them in their weakened state. They also killed many *indios* of the youth's nation who came carrying the precious metal (he mentioned up to twenty loads). He had been spared because he was young. They also killed Ayolas's guide, García's former slave, because he told them that, should Christians come, he would tell them about what the Payagoas had done. The youth was hiding from the Payagoas because he did not want to live with them; now he is here with me. He knew up to twelve Christians by their names. The Payagoas that I had taken prisoner were very sorry to see him; in the end, they agreed with him about everything. With this news, I came down to this port of Asunción because I knew from Your Majesty's officials that the people of Buenos Aires had no more than one hundred fifty measures of corn, and if the harvest should fail, their lives would be in peril.

I gathered as many supplies as I could in this land. In the month of August of the said year, I sent everything with Juan de Ortega on two loaded brigantines to Buenos Aires. Thus, if Your Majesty had decided to send help, the people that came would not die of hunger and for lack of ships in the port of Buenos Aires, as is often the case, being, as it is, desolate land.[30]

30. The geography of the Río de la Plata estuary prevents heavy ships from navigating the several miles of shallow swamp to dock and unload. Rather, smaller boats from the port were needed to unload large vessels. If there were no boats in Buenos

In the meantime, at the time when the *veedor* Alonso Cabrera came from the island of Santa Catalina, I was informed that Gonzalo de Mendoza—who had gone for supplies for the people of Buenos Aires—had brought with him a local *indio principal*, baptized as Domingo by the *comisario* of San Francisco,[31] along with his nephew Miguel. I sent them by García's route back to their homeland, so they could take my report about the situation in these lands to the said *comisario*. For some reason, Domingo turned back halfway, sending instead his nephew Miguel to said island. Apparently, Miguel met Cabeza de Vaca near the sea and guided him back here [to Asunción].

At harvest time, with as many supplies as I could carry, I went with three ships to the said port of Buenos Aires at the end of January of the year 1541. I stayed there until the month of June of said year, waiting for a fleet to come.[32]

Seeing that winter was coming and that it was too late for a fleet to come that year; and fearing that the ship that had left to inform Your Majesty could be lost (for it had been two years since it had left and there had been no news of it); and considering that we had to rely on our own strength, and that many people were sick from the last *entrada* (besides fifty who had already died), and that it was necessary to do an *entrada* before losing our remaining ships, ammunition, and strength in order to get some gold and silver to send to Your Majesty and to find out for certain what had happened to Juan de Ayolas; even as a small ship was being built on the Paraguay so that we might inform Your Majesty of what had happened and about the state of the land, I decided to take the strongest people that were left in the port of Buenos Aires, leaving up to sixty men who were not as hardy.

Considering that the land is very cold and the people there very bellicose, the *veedor* Alonso Cabrera, who was there at the time, requested that I leave eighty men so arrayed that they could support themselves, and if not, to gather all the people in Paraguay, because it was more convenient for everyone's survival. I sought the opinion

---

Aires, the travelers from Spain would have been stranded on their ships and perished. At the time Ortega went to Buenos Aires, Irala did not know whether any fleet from Spain had been sent. In fact, Cabeza de Vaca would soon arrive.

31. Head of the Franciscan mission.

32. Though he mentions Cabeza de Vaca's arrival in the previous paragraph, at this time Irala still did not know that the new governor was en route.

of the clerics and captains and other veterans that were there. The majority of them thought that the people needed to be brought up here, both because we were too few to sustain ourselves divided and because of the lack of clothes and other things, which could be better remedied in Paraguay, which is a warmer land where there is cotton. More so since the Spaniards remaining in these provinces at the time were three hundred fifty men including the clerics, the old, and the sick. And considering that in the service of Your Majesty and for everyone's survival—as by Don Pedro de Mendoza's mandate—it was convenient for us to come together, I decided to bring all the people up here [to Asunción], leaving written instructions in many places, both in letters and on signs and stones, explaining what the people Your Majesty might be served to send to this province needed to do, and disclosing some of the reasons why we had to join together. And so that they would be more willing to follow us and look for us, I omitted from my report what had happened to Juan de Ayolas, and I said that we had in our hands much gold and silver (as I believe God would have granted had Governor Juan de Ayolas returned safely). Likewise, I left on the island of San Gabriel a wooden shack where I put five hundred measures of corn and beans that were left from what I needed for my journey, so that if anyone who came along were to need it, they would find it at hand.

Having come to Paraguay on September 2 of the said year, I immediately set about refurbishing and repairing the ships that were old and building others to set out with two hundred men and local *indios* to discover what I have told Your Majesty. When I was almost ready to begin my journey, on the day of Saint Matthias of 1542,[33] an *indio* came on foot with a letter from Cabeza de Vaca. In it he informed me that Your Majesty had granted us the favor of sending assistance. Cabeza de Vaca intended to send down the Paraná to the mouth of this Paraguay River half of his people, who were tired from the journey. Thus, he requested that I help him with ships for this purpose, as well as assist him in crossing the Paraná because he feared those *indios* whom he knew were not our friends. Therefore, I immediately sent Garci Venegas[34] with three of the ships that I had

33. The feast day of the apostle Matthias was originally celebrated on February 24; it has since been moved to May 14.

34. García Venegas, *tesorero* and one of Irala's staunchest allies. He was sent to escort Cabeza de Vaca back to Spain in 1545.

repaired and the necessary supplies. Venegas found the men that the said Cabeza de Vaca had sent down the Paraná in canoes. They were in dire need of supplies and rescue because, uniting to kill them, the local *indios* had attacked them with bows and arrows. They would have been killed before the arrival of the brigantines if a friendly *indio*, who had been Gonzalo de Acosta's slave and had been there since the time of Diego García,[35] had not helped them by providing supplies. At the same time, in preparation for the arrival of the said Cabeza de Vaca, I sent by land a Christian interpreter with *indio* allies to clear the roads and to provide them with food and all kinds of service.

Cabeza de Vaca arrived here on March 12 of the said year. He showed us a *provisión* from Your Majesty ordering that, in the event of Governor Juan de Ayolas's death, he should be obeyed as governor of this land. The only reliable information we had about Juan de Ayolas's death was what the young Chane had said. However, he could still be alive since the Chane said that there were still Christians left in his land, one of whom might be Ayolas; thus, we did not accept this command. Cabeza de Vaca showed another *provisión* in which Your Majesty ordered that in case of doubt regarding whether Juan de Ayolas was dead or alive, we were to accept him in the name of Your Majesty as Ayolas's lieutenant. Once we had seen it, it was quickly obeyed and he was received according to those *provisiones*. As soon as he arrived, Cabeza de Vaca asked me to help him send ships to Buenos Aires to rescue the people on the ship coming by sea from the Island of Santa Catalina. Seeing how convenient it was for Your Majesty's service and the well-being of this land, I prepared two of the aforementioned ships, loaded them with supplies at my expense, and sent them to help said people. Once the rescue ships had left, I had a large new brigantine made from the timber and planks that I had at that time. I had it loaded and sent it with the other brigantines to rescue the people on said ship; these supplies and those that I had left [on the island of San Gabriel] helped them survive.

I went back to preparing the other two ships I had. Then, with another new ship that Cabeza de Vaca had made (which was loaded with supplies at my expense), on the twentieth of October of said year, Cabeza de Vaca sent me and ninety-three men upriver to

35. From 1528 to 1529.

discover inhabited land from which to stage an *entrada* to the western part of this river. The intent was to avoid what had allegedly happened to Juan de Ayolas on his return through deserted lands. I found such land at sixteen and a half degrees. It was better supplied than what we had seen thus far, and the people were more civilized, because each person lived in his own house. I found among them many *indios* who had been Garcia's slaves and had arrived after the Guaraní killed him. I traveled with them three days inland to talk to some Guaraní *indios* who were on certain hills warring with all the other nations. I found out from the Guaraní that inhabited land was about fifteen days away, that García had crossed that desert, that García's men had killed and destroyed many people in that land, and that the rest had taken refuge in other villages further inland, which was said to be very populated. Since I was not commissioned to travel more than three days inland, after learning all this I returned to inform Cabeza de Vaca, leaving the land at peace.

As I made my way back, Cabeza de Vaca sent me a letter requesting that, if possible, I execute Aracare, an *indio principal* who was thirty leagues from this port, because to do so would serve Your Majesty. I followed his orders and informed him about what had happened upon my return. In the meantime, the town[36] had burned down with all its supplies, so Cabeza de Vaca found it necessary to send one hundred men with a certain Gonzalo de Mendoza as captain to the port they call Gijuy. Upon his return, Mendoza informed Cabeza de Vaca that the whole land had risen up in arms because of the death of the said *principal* Aracare. Consequently, Cabeza de Vaca sent me with one hundred men to pacify the land and to bring it once again to Your Majesty's obedience. I was able to do so, though with much labor and peril to my person. It was first necessary to destroy two towns that were defended by very strong palisades and that had more than seven or eight thousand *indios* inside; four Christians were killed and forty more were wounded. Leaving everything at peace and all the lands' *indios principales* subjected to Your Majesty's obedience, I came down to this port to give an account of everything.

Cabeza de Vaca left from this port to make his *entrada* with ten sails and four hundred men on the day of Our Lady in September of 1543. On the way, all the said *indios* who had rebelled came out to

---

36. Asunción, where a major fire broke out in February 1543.

greet him and to bring him food. He entered the port of Los Reyes,[37] where he found all the *indios* at peace. They received him very well, bringing much food, and gave him *indios* to carry his supplies inland. After eleven days, he turned around and returned to the said port. From there he sent a brigantine with fifty men upriver to find out about a nation called Xarayes, where I had heard there was precious metal. At the same time he ordered attacks on some nearby *indios*. As things stood, all the people got so sick that there were only two healthy men in all the camp. I believe it was because of the water that we drank, which came from a lagoon. Due to this and because of an official request by Your Majesty's *contador* Felipe de Cáceres, Cabeza de Vaca came down to this port, where he arrived on Wednesday of Holy Week of 1544. Your Majesty's officials and all the people considered that he often overstepped his authority regarding Your Majesty's service and the pacification of the land, and that he had not fulfilled Your Majesty's orders. Thus, they seized him and are on their way to inform of everything, with him as prisoner. Meanwhile, considering that it was in the interest of Your Majesty's service and the pacification of the land, they requested that I accept the post of lieutenant governor, which I formerly held, until receiving commands to the contrary from Your Majesty. They also requested that the captains, *regidores,* and all the people choose whom they wanted, and they elected me. And so I remain, in Your Majesty's name, preparing ships to do an *entrada* with three hundred men and fifteen hundred *indio* allies, through which I hope to be of great service to Your Majesty and earn a great victory. For this I have made saltpeter with much labor and expense, which should allow us to refine the little gunpowder that we have left and to make more.

The most necessary things that by Your Majesty's command ought to be provided for this land are plenty of good and fine powder, guns (though not the kind that fire buckshot), and cross-bows, and string for rope, and tar and ample cloth, and shoes, and house linen for the people, and especially a doctor and an apothecary with all kinds of medicine.

And since the needs of the body are nothing without those of the soul, Your Majesty must provide a priest for the church, for clerics as well as for laypeople; one whose life, teaching, and example will

---

37. Site of his aforementioned *entrada.*

garner respect and humility, and let Your Majesty's royal conscience be at peace.

May Our Lord keep and increase Your Sacred, Cesarean, Catholic person with many more kingdoms and lordships. From Paraguay, March 1, 1545.

Your Majesty's humble vassal who kisses you royal hands and feet,
Domingo de Irala.

Francisco Galán to Rodrigo de Vera (March 1, 1545)

The author of this letter is not the lieutenant governor of Buenos Aires, but a man whose name is a near homonym of "Francisco Ruiz Galán."[38] The envelope identifies the intended recipient as Rodrigo de Vera de Villavicencio, *alcalde* of the town of Zahara, probably the one called de la Sierra; it lies northwest of Jerez de la Frontera.[39] Galán appears to have been very well connected. The surnames of the addresses and of the people he mentions in closing—de Vera, Villavicencio, Estopiñán, and Núñez—identify them as members of the most prestigious and powerful lineages in Jerez, all of which were interrelated by marriage (see Bustos Rodríguez 1985). They were also related to Álvar Núñez Cabeza de Vaca, whose father was Francisco de Vera.[40] Galán's allegiance to this clan correlates to the tenor of the letter, which was presented as evidence in the legal proceedings that Cabeza de Vaca initiated as soon as he got back to Spain against the men who had deposed him.[41]

Francisco Galán explains that the loss of Pedro de Mendoza's fleet was due to the lack of experience of the captains who, moreover, misgoverned and mismanaged the early settlement of the Río de la

---

38. Archivo General de Indias, justicia. Autos fiscales. Charcas. Justicia, 1130.

39. On the coast southwest of Jerez is another town named Zahara, called de los Atunes, which is a small fishing village.

40. Galán's addressee may be Francisco de Vera's younger brother; the recurrence of identical names across family lines and generations hinders precise identification.

41. The extant text is a copy preserved as part of a *probanza*, or affidavit of testimony; the cover sheet specifies that it was presented before the *alcalde* of Jerez on October 7, 1545.

Plata. This epistle complements Domingo de Irala's letter by adding a number of revealing details that shed a different light on the facts that they both provide. Galán confirms that legal procedures were consistently followed, but he also calls them into question by suggesting that many inquiries were conducted merely for the sake of form. Thus, everything that these two documents offer by way of explanation of the events that took place must be taken with a grain of salt. On the other hand, they show how human passion underlay both the achievements and the failures of the Río de la Plata's conquest and colonization. Whereas Domingo de Irala's letter gives the sense of fait accompli with a hint of irony, Galán's conveys one of regret with more than a touch of pathos.

This letter illustrates how the legal process was followed strictly but manipulated, so that it was ultimately unreliable. As suggested by Galán, the bias of the witnesses undercut the alleged trustworthiness of conducting a legal proceeding. Moreover, rampant prevarication undermined the value of the legal process not only for doing justice but also as a record of what actually happened. Any measure of historical accuracy can be achieved only by comparing the greatest possible number of documents.

———————•◆•———————

Magnificent Lord,

As Your Honor knows, since coming to this difficult and dangerous land in the company of Don Pedro de Mendoza, I have not written Your Honor to tell about the misfortunes that have happened here since then. It has not been for lack of will or desire—because those I have never lacked, nor will I, regarding your service—but because I have not had the means. Every time that there has been a messenger from this land and province, I have been absent from the port of Buenos Aires, from whence ships set sail for those kingdoms of Spain. This has caused me great sorrow because Your Honor will have regarded me as careless and negligent; since it was out of my hands, I beg Your Honor to restore to me my credit.

When Don Pedro came to this land, there were many deaths, as much from hunger as from enemies, and the whole fleet was on the verge of being lost and destroyed by the captains' lack of good government and administration, because Mendoza and those who came with him had little experience. And within a few days of the said deaths, Mendoza went upriver in brigantines to the port they call Corpus Christi, which is eighty leagues up the river from the port of Buenos Aires. Corpus Christi was the first port, stage, and settlement founded in this province after the port of Buenos Aires.[42]

In this port of Corpus Christi, he was in communication with some *indios* called Tinbues. Here the people recovered and had food. After several days, Mendoza sent Juan de Ayolas as his captain general with some of the people on three ships to explore the Paraguay River in order to discover and to gauge the best land through which to enter. Three months after he left, the said Don Pedro de Mendoza, having retreated and returned to the said port of Buenos Aires, sent Captain Juan de Salazar de Espinoza[43] with two ships in search of the said Juan de Ayolas. At said time I went in his company. On that trip we suffered great and intolerable toils, both from the sailing and from hunger. And after more or less six months, we found in the Paraguay River two of Juan de Ayolas's brigantines with thirty men on them, and a certain Domingo de Irala from Biscay[44] as their captain. Irala informed and said how, on February 12 of the year 1537, from the port of La Candelaria (on this river, where some fisher *indios* called Payaguaes live), the said Juan de Ayolas had entered the land with one hundred thirty men in search of the mines and villages that were inland. He had taken as a guide a slave (formerly owned by a Christian named García)[45] who had gone into the said land and knew the way, as well as a few others of the said Payaguaes. Ayolas had left Irala in the said brigantines to wait for him in said port until his return. Having heard this account, the said captain Juan de Salazar went down this Paraguay River one hundred twenty leagues from the said port of La Candelaria. And in agreement with these Cario *indios* he established a wooden fort[46] that lies three hundred leagues from the port of Buenos Aires. There he left half the people he had brought and returned in the brigantines to the port of Buenos Aires to report to the said Don Pedro de Mendoza, who, as he discovered,

---

42. Juan de Ayolas founded the fort of Corpus Christi on his first foray upriver.
43. See note 5 in Pedro de Mendoza's letter.
44. Located on Spain's northern coast, the region of Biscay is part of the Basque Country.
45. Alejo García. See note 23 in Domingo de Irala's letter.
46. Asunción, founded by Juan de Salazar on August 15, 1537.

had left for the kingdoms of Spain. Then he returned to the said house and port called Asunción to guard and defend it. As I have told Your Honor, since I have always been in his company, I have not had the chance to inform you about everything that has happened. Last year, 1539, Alonso Cabrera, His Majesty's *veedor*, came to this port of Asunción. And since his coming, this land has never lacked revolt and scandals, which, as a quarrelsome and restless man, he has caused and sought. He imposed new taxes on the people, taking undue fifths[47] and tariffs, misinterpreting a *provisión* that he brought from His Majesty. And he made and promoted the said Domingo de Irala to lieutenant governor and captain general, even though he does not possess the qualities required of a person who would hold and exercise such titles. This and other worse and more consequential things the said Alonso Cabrera did in order to rule and so that we would all be governed by his whim.

After being instated as lieutenant governor, around December of the said year, the said Captain Domingo de Irala left this port with nine brigantines, two hundred eighty Christians, and some Cario *indios*. I found myself in this *entrada*. We went in search of the said Captain Juan de Ayolas. And we went to the port of San Sebastián,[48] which lays seven or eight leagues downriver from where the said Juan de Ayolas went inland. Around February of 1540, the said Captain Domingo de Irala and his people went inland from here, leaving the ships safely at port. He was inland for nineteen days, and because he found the land all swampy and covered with water, he was forced to retreat to where they had left the brigantines. Having returned, the said Captain Domingo de Irala questioned five Payaguaes that he had seized before going inland (two of which were known to have been guides taken by the said Juan de Ayolas). The *indios* said and declared how Juan de Ayolas had gone inland as far as the land of a people called Chanes, whereabouts he acquired much gold and silver. They also said that he had returned to the said port of La Candelaria with the *indios* Chanes carrying the said gold and silver. When he arrived, he did not find the brigantines or the people that he left at the said

47. The crown was owed 20 percent, the royal fifth, of all precious metals found, traded, mined, or plundered.

48. The port at San Sebastián was established by Domingo de Irala as a launching stage for an expedition inland with the goal of finding Ayolas, as well as a passable northwesterly route toward the Sierra de la Plata.

port, which caused the said Juan de Ayolas and all the Christians in his company great disheartenment. And they also told of how they had made houses and lean-tos from straw to stay there until the said brigantines returned. They waited for a month, at the end of which the Payaguaes, greedy to possess the metals that the said Juan de Ayolas had brought, made a great gathering of their people and others nearby. And after the said gathering, the Payaguae leaders entreated the said Juan de Ayolas and the Christians to go with them to their houses, where they would be served and fed. Considering the friendship and good deeds that they had done for him at the time of his departure, the said Juan de Ayolas acquiesced. So they geared up and began walking with them. And one day, as they were walking, with the sun up high, and nearing the houses of the said Payaguaes, the said *indios'* ambush came out of nowhere. Suddenly they fell upon them, and in a short time, Juan de Ayolas was killed along with all the Christians and the *indios* Chanes who were with him and who were beaten to death; they took all the gold and silver he had. When the said Captain Domingo de Irala heard of this, he ordered all the people to embark and to return to this port of Asunción. And as they were embarking, a young *indio* whose semblance seemed that of a slave came swimming. He said he was a Chane and that he had come with the said Juan de Ayolas. He declared in detail Ayolas's *entrada* and return, as well as his death, which was as I have stated above. This *indio* said that along the road he had buried some gold, and the rest had been taken by the *indios* Payaguaes when they killed them; he had escaped and avoided death by fleeing to some trees, where he was later found by the said Payaguaes and seized. Learning that there were Christians in the said port and river, he fled from the Payaguaes and came to join the company of the Christians. With this new information, we returned to this port of Asunción, where many people got sick as soon as we arrived, and some of them died from the excessive toil that we had suffered.

After this happened around January of the year of 1541, the said Captain Vergara[49] went downriver to the port of Buenos Aires, where there were people who could reinforce this conquest. As soon as he arrived, at the behest of and in agreement with the said Alonso Cabrera, he had the port dismantled and sent all the people to this

---

49. Domingo de Irala, sometimes referred to as "Vergara" in reference to the city where he was born.

port of Asunción. He did this to wrong us and so that if someone should come from Spain or a stray ship should reach the said port, there would be no safe anchorage. I do not write further to Your Honor about these and more grievous deeds that have been done in this land for the lack of paper there is here.

Once in Asunción, Captain Domingo de Irala decided to undertake an *entrada,* and as he was preparing it, Governor Álvar Núñez Cabeza de Vaca came to this city. As he arrived, he was received by His Majesty's officials and captains. He immediately decided to inquire and find out from where to explore and gauge the land so he could conquer it. And as he was preparing the necessary ships, he had some dissentions with His Majesty's officials because he prevented the collection of the fifths and the miserable things they charged for. In light of this, the said officials decided to send two Franciscan friars to the coast of Brazil to inform His Majesty of what had happened. Seeing that the officials were stirring up the land and impeding his exploration, the governor ordered the said friars to return and had the officials seized for certain irreverent things they said and did. He tried them and sent them to His Majesty.

Having sent them away, on the day of Our Lady in September 1543, Cabeza de Vaca departed with ten ships, four hundred men, and ten horses. Leaving this land secure, he went to the port of Los Reyes.[50] From Los Reyes, by way of a people called Coronucocies, he traveled inland for nineteen days until he reached certain *indios* that he found along the road, from whom he found out about the villages in the region. And since they told him that the villages that had food were far away, he had to retreat. And before he left, he sent six Christians and some *indios* to see and to explore the said villages, while he returned to where he had left the brigantines.

A few days later, the people he had sent to see the said land returned. And having been informed about the news they brought, as he was preparing to go inland again, most of the people fell ill with fever. This illness was so widespread that even the governor got sick. Realizing that the said disease was serious, the governor decided to return to this port of Asunción. Fifteen days after his return, bedridden as he was, on the day of our lord San Marcos[51] in 1544, the

---

50. The port from which Cabeza de Vaca attempted his *entrada.*
51. The feast day of Saint Mark is April 25.

said officials, moved by their hatred, went armed with their friends and supporters to the governor's house and seized him. After they seized him, saying slanderous and ugly things to him, there was a great uproar and scandal. They seized the *alcalde mayor* and *alguaciles*, insulting them greatly as they dragged them, and shaved their beards, and took away their rods of office, which they withheld from the governor in the name of His Majesty. They released the prisoners. They did other very serious and atrocious things that were a disservice to God and to His Majesty. Not satisfied with this, they imprisoned Cabeza de Vaca, barricading the streets and houses, setting a guard so that by day and by night he would be thus guarded, which is a tremendous thing to witness and to describe. They read in public and published a defamatory libel. They instated a lieutenant governor and captain general who named an *alcalde* and *alguaciles*, who conducted their inquiries through their bribed friends and supporters, hence the perjury that will be revealed [in Spain]. They have persecuted the loyal vassals of His Majesty, who have zealously looked out for the interests of His Majesty's service. Regarding these things, they have done atrocious things worthy of great punishment: not satisfied with persecuting the laypersons who spoke in benefit of God and king, they have imprisoned an ordained priest, and have kept him between four walls for eight months. To hear the blasphemies and to see the lack of respect for God and His Majesty in this land at this time is enough to make one cry.

The loyal vassals meant to free the governor. I assure Your Honor that they were so determined that they would have done it were it not for the fact that, as it happened, four friends of the said officials' allies (one of whom was the *tesorero* García de Venegas de Córdoba)[52] have sworn to kill the governor if they see anyone rise up to free him. Besides, the governor told us through one of his guards to settle down because they threatened him every day, telling him to confess, pointing daggers at his chest, saying they would kill him if he did not tell his friends not to revolt. In view of the uproar and upheaval that have already happened, we believe that the governor may be more dead than alive, because since they locked him up, none of his friends or His Majesty's servants has seen him. I leave out other more significant things because there Your Honor will be informed at length

52. See note 34 in Domingo de Irala's letter.

by Pedro Hernández, His Majesty's notary in this province, who has seen everything that has happened in this land since the coming of Don Pedro de Mendoza. I beg Your Honor to give him full credit, as his person deserves, because he is a man who will say nothing but the truth. And to the extent that Your Honor can favor him, I beg Your Honor to do so, as he is a gentleman and a friend.

Sir, as soon as his lordship the governor arrived, he did me the honor of asking about me owing to Your Honor's gracious recommendation. May the Lord grant that I return in time to serve and to repay Your Honor for these and future services, as I wish.

The lord governor has told me how the archdeacon is deceased and God took him (may he be in His glory). A thousand kisses for the hands of my lady Doña Catalina de Estopiñán, to whose prayers I commend myself. I kiss the hands of Their Honors Francisco de Villavicencio and Pedro Núñez. May the Lord keep and increase Your Honor's magnificent person so that you may serve Him for many years. From this city of Asunción, March 1, 1545.

> *Kissing the hands of Your Honor,*
> *Francisco Galán.*

Juan Pavón to Martín de Agreda (June 15, 1556)

As stated in his letter, Juan Pavón fought for the crown against the *comuneros* when they revolted against the newly enthroned Holy Roman Emperor Charles V in 1520–21. Later, he served as *alguacil mayor* of Écija, a city located in southern Spain. He joined Pedro de Mendoza's expedition to the Río de la Plata, where he was appointed *alcalde* of Buenos Aires. Later, he was named *alcalde mayor* of Asunción by Álvar Núñez Cabeza de Vaca, to whom he remained loyal. Pavón was kept imprisoned for his fidelity until after the second *adelantado*'s forced departure.

In 1556, Pavón wrote to the *licenciado* Martín de Agreda, *procurador* of the Council of the Indies, to demand justice for the iniquities committed against him and for other excesses perpetrated by Domingo de Irala and his supporters.[53] The letter underscores that

---

53. Archivo Histórico Nacional, Colección Documentos de Indias, diversoscolecciones, 24, N.9.

the addressee does not know the author, yet the latter expects the former to comply with his request to render him justice. The letter suggests a seemingly blind faith in the Spanish administration, a confidence in the power of personal testimony, and a sincere belief in the righteousness of the author's own cause.

The tenor of Pavón's letter reflects the fact that he was a career official with a history of service. As befits a former *alcalde mayor*, he is very concerned with legal issues. The letter explains pointedly and succinctly how justice had been abused and how the symbols of authority, namely, the rod of office, had been disregarded. Moreover, Pavón was forced to endure a significant affront to his honor as a gentleman by having his beard shorn.

<hr>

Most Magnificent Lord,

The fact that Your Honor does not know me or have any knowledge of me will not prevent me from informing Your Honor of my actions and those of others during this conquest after the imprisonment of Álvar Núñez Cabeza de Vaca and of myself, his chief magistrate in this province. On the night that Governor Álvar Núñez Cabeza de Vaca was seized, I was seized with him, and they took the king's staff from my hands, and they gave me a good beating and shaved my beard, and they dragged me to Alonso Cabrera's house, where they were holding the said governor, whereupon thirty or forty armed men came out to greet me. The leader was Felipe de Cáceres, His Majesty's *contador*, and when they arrived with me they told him, "Here we have him. What do you want us to do with him?" Cabrera replied, "Take him to the jail, and put his head in the stocks, and keep him overnight." They freed two thieves that I had imprisoned and threw me in in their place. Your Honor, see how they treat one of His Majesty's justices. They also freed a man who was sentenced to death for killing another. The following morning, they took me from the jail to the house of Domingo de Irala, who was second in command, and they put me in a locked chamber with three men to guard me. I did not see the light of day for the eleven months and eighteen days that I was imprisoned there until they took Governor Cabeza de Vaca to Spain and released me from prison. For all this, I wish to lay criminal charges with His Majesty and Your Honor, in his royal name, and for any other crimes that should come to light, I demand justice, justice, justice, sir.

I will now tell Your Honor about some things that have happened in this land. After the governor had been taken to Spain, they announced an *entrada*. They went inland and depopulated all the land from here to Peru, killing the *indios* and taking them as slaves. Irala left Don Francisco de Mendoza as his lieutenant in this city. I do not know why Don Francisco renounced Irala's authority. At the sound of the bell, the majority of the people gathered in the church and they elected a gentleman from Seville named Diego d'Abrego to govern in the name of His Majesty. As this gentleman was in charge when Domingo de Irala returned from the *entrada*, he demanded his obedience. Irala responded that he would give him a response: the next day, Irala sent for him in order to give his response, and seized him. D'Abrego escaped from his imprisonment and fled to the hills. There, Irala seized him again, as well as other gentlemen who were with him. They brought them all with their hands shackled and imprisoned them; he escaped once again. Meanwhile, Irala undertook his *entrada* again, leaving Felipe de Cáceres, His Majesty's *contador*, in his stead.

There was much discord in the town about whether an elected official could select another without His Majesty's authority to govern or select him. Irala wanted to hang some people for speaking about it. He desisted and proceeded with his *entrada*. Some people went to d'Abrego, who was on the run for fear of the said Irala. Others were of the opinion that since d'Abrego had been elected, he should govern. The town was scandalized over this. The said Irala had to return with his men to pursue d'Abrego; he seized and hanged three men. Some he could not capture, but he took their property and distributed it among his friends and supporters. To fight this battle, he brought in and used a nation of *indios* who were enemies of the locals. Irala went back to the *entrada* that he had begun. He left the said Felipe de Cáceres in command. Cáceres issued and signed an order, which was countersigned by Bartolomé González (notary public of the *cabildo*), for his constable Antón Martín Escaso to kill the said Diego d'Abrego wherever he could take him. The said constable made it public and scouted d'Abrego out. Escaso took certain friends of his and, at the dawn watch, approached d'Abrego as he lay sick in his bed and blind in his eyes. Escaso shot him with a crossbow, piercing his heart and lungs, and his body from side to side, so he did not even have the chance to say "God save me." Those who go to Spain will inform Your Honor more thoroughly of everything that took place.[54]

Your Honor, attend to how things are dispatched to this land from there, and alert the president [of the Council] that we already know what has been decided there a year or a year and a half before the decisions are sent. Domingo de Irala returned from the *entrada* he had begun because of many divisions among them; a great number of the *indio* allies died. Bartolomé Justiniano came here with *provisiones* from His Majesty for Domingo Martinez d'Irala to be governor until His Majesty should decide otherwise. A year and more before Justiniano's arrival, we had copies of the *provisiones* and letters, telling Irala to distribute the land and to embark on his exploration and *entrada*. Once Bartolomé Justiniano arrived, he presented his *provisiones*, and Irala received and obeyed them to the letter: he had been distributing the land for two or three months by the time they came. He distributed as he saw fit, taking from the old conquistadors and giving to those who came fleeing from Peru because of the Viceroy's death and for having fought against His Majesty's royal standard,[55] and also giving to, among others, French and Britons who are in this land.[56] There Your Honor will be informed and discover the truth about how the land was distributed.

Once the land was all distributed, Irala left this city with fifty of his friends for San Vicente,[57] land of the king of Portugal. Twenty or thirty days after he left, the bishop came on Ash Wednesday. It was necessary to send for Irala two or three times. I will say no more about this case. Those who will inform Your Honor copiously, truthfully, and at length are on their way.

54. Pavón is referring to a group of conquistadors who were able to return to Spain in 1556 on the ship that had brought Bishop Pedro de la Torre to the Río de la Plata.

55. The *encomenderos* of Peru revolted when Viceroy Blasco Núñez Vela (1495–1546) attempted to enforce a new set of laws meant to curtail the *encomienda* system. Núñez Vela was deposed in 1544 and later beheaded after a failed attempt to wrest power from Gonzalo Pizarro (1502–48). The rebellion was quelled by Pedro de la Gasca (1493–1567), who had Pizarro executed. Some of Pizarro's supporters may have escaped to Paraguay to avoid a similar fate.

56. Pavón speaks of "franceses y bretones." The use of these terms may be generic, meaning "enemy foreigners," rather than specific.

57. San Vicente (São Vicente) was the first permanent settlement established by the Portuguese in Brazil, near present-day Santos, on the coast south of São Paulo.

Sir, I am an old man who in Spain had much honor. I was Blasco Núñez Vela's chief constable in the city of Écija, Malaga. I served His Majesty with arms and horse. I fought in two battles, one in Villalar against the *comuneros*,[58] and another with the governors in Pamplona against the French.[59] I spent my estate to join Don Pedro de Mendoza in this conquest. I was Juan de Ayolas's lieutenant, then Cabeza de Vaca's *alcade mayor*. Irala has taken away all this because I am not in his good graces. I ask the president [of the Council] that His Highness grant me the position of faithful executor, with a vote in the *cabildo*, for the position is vacant and not appointed. I beg Your Honor to be my advocate for the sake of my old age, for I am old and I am tired of the troubles that they have caused and continue to cause me. And I have served His Majesty twenty-two years.

May Our Lord bless and keep Your Honor's splendid person as Your Honor wishes, with great status and dignity. From this city of Asunción, the fifteenth of June of the year 1556.

Sir, I beg this of Your Honor as a service to God. May Your Honor arrange this for me though I have not served Your Honor, who does not know me. I will assume that Your Honor does me this favor and as such I will receive it.

Your Honor's true servant who kisses your hands.
Juan Pavón

Francisco de Andrada to the Council of the Indies (March 1, 1545)

The religious conversion of the natives provided the ostensible justification of the Spanish conquest, and the first missionaries saw themselves as key agents in its success. Their responsibilities included providing religious services and spiritual guidance for Spanish

58. The Revolt of the *Comuneros* against Charles V took place in Castile between 1520 and 1521. Taking advantage of the emperor's absence, the city councils of Castile rose up in arms, seeking to put his mother Juana, known as *la Loca*, the madwoman, on the throne. The revolt was defeated a few months after the emperor's supporters won a decisive victory against the *comuneros* at the Battle of Villalar on April 23, 1521. See Elliot (2002, 151–60).

59. The Battle of Pamplona took place on May 20, 1521. Supported by the French, troops from Navarre managed to defeat Spanish forces as part of an ultimately unsuccessful attempt to liberate the small kingdom from the Spanish crown's authority.

conquistadors and settlers. More important, they were responsible for bringing the natives into the fold of Catholicism. The letter written by Francisco de Andrada, who was a secular priest, reflects both ongoing concern about the (im)moral behavior of Spaniards in Asunción and a general preoccupation with the natives' religious instruction.[60] Remarkably, it omits any mention of the political drama that unfolded at the time of Governor Cabeza de Vaca's imprisonment. The missionaries' most fundamental assumption was that the conversion of the natives was God's will. Thus, any event that delayed or enabled the work of evangelization could be construed as providential in nature. The biblical overtones of Andrada's description of a plague of locusts and the subsequent bounty of fish correspond to this interpretative frame. On the other hand, his portrayal of the natives echoes a common missionary perspective that presented lack as an asset for conversion. Andrada explains that the Guaraní did not have idols, kings, or gold but only a few meager possessions. In other words, they had nothing that would prevent them from accepting Christianity.[61] On the contrary, he portrays them as eager learners, anxious to join the community of the faithful. Missionaries' accounts often underscored the natives' aptitude and enthusiasm for conversion as a way of bolstering support for their activities. The complementary image of the natives as cannibalistic and incestuous was a transparent device for underscoring the need for missionary work.

In contrast with the mostly virtuous Guaraní, the Spaniards are characterized by their vices. However, they are not the vicious wolves of more polemic accounts, like the one by the cleric Martín González. Andrada focuses on the conquistadors' sexual promiscuity, measured by the large number of *mestizo* children running around in Asunción. However, the cleric partly shifts blame by stressing the important role played by women in Guaraní society, which forced each Spaniard to take several Guaraní women as food providers—and concubines. Andrada's relatively mild criticism, as well as his omission of any political controversy, is undoubtedly related to the fact that he was one of the *conquistadores viejos* and that he was on

---

60. Archivo General de Indias, Autos fiscales. Charcas, Justicia, 1131.

61. The most famous representative of this view is Bartolomé de la Casas, who also stressed the *indios'* simplicity, gentleness, and humility. For a succinct appreciation of Las Casas, see Brading (1993, 58–78).

good terms with Domingo de Irala. Andrada arrived to the Río de la Plata on Pedro de Mendoza's fleet and was appointed town chaplain soon after the founding of Asunción. He approved the deposition of Governor Cabeza de Vaca in 1544. Afterward, he acted as mediator between Irala and the remaining *leales*; years later, he acted as the executor of Governor Irala's last will (Lafuente Machaín 1943, 49). The denunciation of the Spaniards' conduct, together with his repeated (i.e., ineffective) rebukes, contributes to Andrada's self-portrayal as a defender of propriety. At the same time, the friar casts himself as an effective evangelist by highlighting his adherence to church protocols and the success of his teaching among the Guaraní. Long-standing tradition established that adult converts needed to have a basic understanding of the faith before being admitted into the Catholic Church through the sacrament of baptism.[62] To guarantee comprehension, teaching had to be done in the native language. Andrada notes that the son of Captain Gonzalo de Acosta, who spoke Spanish and Guaraní, translated for him.[63] Though the accuracy of the translation is impossible to gauge, Andrada underscores the enthusiasm with which the Guaraní attended to his words to indicate the success of his preaching. However, what prompted the cleric to begin baptizing his native flock was the appearance of a competitor, the shaman Entigura. Andrada's apprehension was judicious: indigenous revolts in the Río de la Plata were often led by signing shamans who challenged the missionaries' spiritual authority.[64]

Baptism was a prerequisite for marriage, which was also encouraged by the missionaries as a key component of their efforts to Christianize indigenous society. Yet, in the case of monogamous marriage, it is not hard to perceive in Andrada's letter the give and

62. Teaching as an aspect of evangelization appears in the Gospels and the Acts of the Apostles; Acts 18:11, for instance, states that "Paul stayed in Corinth for a year and a half, teaching them the word of God" (New International Version). Baptism provoked controversy among the missionaries. The early Franciscans were proponents of expediency, which included performing mass baptisms. In contrast, Dominicans believed that formal indoctrination was a prerequisite. Secular clergy shared the latter belief, which was consistent with their view of the Church as an institution made up of laws and codified procedures (Schwaller 2011, 267).

63. The interpreter's name may have been Gregorio de Acosta and his knowledge of Guaraní the result of having lived for several years on the Brazilian coast with his father. See the section on guides and interpreters above.

64. On the correlation and competition between Franciscan friars and Guaraní shamans, see Necker (1979).

take between imported beliefs and local customs. In his instructions to the natives, Andrada maintains that a man can only have one wife, and that he must marry her in the church, but he later concedes that other women will continue to share a married man's household.[65] The missionaries to the Río de la Plata were never in a position to impose the Catholic dogma, not even in the friar-managed communities, whose organization was based on slightly modified Guaraní social and economic practices. The strategy of accommodation that the Franciscans instituted in the first missions was maintained by the Jesuits when they took charge of evangelization work in the seventeenth century (Necker 1979, 241). At every stage, the Guaraní helped shape the terms of their engagement with the missionaries (Ganson 2005, 29).

Like most letters addressed to the king, Andrada's missive includes a series of petitions. The cleric asks for cult paraphernalia to dignify his church; he also wishes to be named bishop and allowed to keep a portion of the tithe to support himself and his family. These requests are addressed to the crown because the king was also the executive head and formal sponsor of the Catholic Church in the New World by virtue of the *Patronato Real*. The evangelical responsibility of the Spanish monarchs dated to 1493, when Pope Alexander VI (1431–1503) granted them dominion over newly discovered territories.[66] In 1501, the pope allowed the Spanish crown to keep the tithe collected from New World churches so that more could be founded and endowed. Royal authority over the missionary church was further enhanced in 1508 after Pope Julius II granted the *Patronato Real* to the kings of Spain. As royal patron, the king had control over practically every aspect of religious activity in the New World, including

---

65. Polygamy was an especially vexing problem for church authorities throughout the New World. In the Viceroyalty of Peru, it was addressed by the First Council of Lima (1551–52), which condemned polygamy along with concubinage. Held in the wake of the Council of Trent (1545–63), the Second Council of Lima (1567–68) reiterated the prohibition against these practices but was more decisive in the enactment of its decrees. However, enforcing monogamy outside colonial hubs was difficult. On the various councils' resolutions, see Vargas Ugarte (1951–54).

66. The pope claimed the authority to do so as the vicar of Christ, who was the king of the world. This reasoning was later criticized by theologians such as the Dominican Francisco de Vitoria (1492–1546), who argued that Christ's kingdom was not of this world and, therefore, the pope had no authority to decide worldly matters (Brading 1993, 84).

the establishment of dioceses and the appointment of church officials.[67] The *Patronato Real* allowed for a dynamic and well-funded evangelization effort. However, it was also a persistent source of friction between the papacy and the Spanish crown. Moreover, the conflation of civil and religious authority was a common cause of jurisdictional disputes between church prelates and the king's deputies overseas.

Unlike his fellow letter writers, Andrada uses the honorific "Highness" (*Alteza*) rather than "Majesty" (*Majestad*) to address Charles V. The choice may be generational since, as stated in the letter, Andrada was relatively old. "Highness" was the term generally used to address Spanish monarchs until 1519, when "Majesty" became the standard from of address for the newly elected Holy Roman Emperor Charles V.

———◆◆◆———

Most Powerful Lords,

Your Highness[68] should know that I am a poor priest and that I have spent the greater part of my life studying until I was ordained for mass in the holy church of the city of Seville. Examined by the *provisor* who resided there at that time, the *licenciado* Temiño, prior and *canónigo* of the said church, I sang mass and lived there for seven or eight years, until I decided to come to this land with Don Pedro de Mendoza (may he be in God's glory) with the intent of laboring in the field of the Lord, counting on His exalted assistance, knowing that those who call upon Him for matters related to His service are heard. It was not my fault that, when Antonio López departed, I did not relate to Your Highness what I will now tell.[69] Rather, it was because those who went there did not see those of us who were in the land of the Paraguay nor did we see them. Due to the distance of three hundred leagues or more that separated us, little did we know

---

67. The only religious order that was not bound by the terms of the *Patronato Real* was the Society of Jesus, more commonly known as the Jesuit Order; it was officially established in 1540 and answered directly to the pope.

68. Andrada addresses the king through his ministers at the Council of the Indies.

69. Antonio López de Aguiar was the captain of the caravel *Santa Catalina*, which reached Buenos Aires in the spring of 1538. It had sailed from Spain the previous fall, along with the ship *Marañona*, which bore the *veedor* Alonso Cabrera.

that a caravel was sailing to Spain. It is because of this that I have not notified and informed Your Highness about the things that I will speak of in this letter.

After Don Pedro de Mendoza (may he be in God's glory) departed from this land to Spain, most of the people went up to the Paraguay River by ship, in which company I found myself. We disembarked in this port where this town is now settled, which is called the city of Asunción, because its settling and building began on that date.[70] The quality of the land: the soil is poor and there is a lack of food supplies. Nonetheless, it is densely inhabited by naked people. They possess neither gold nor silver; their houses are made of straw; their belongings are a bow and arrows, a cotton net in which they sleep, and tools with which they sow corn, manioc, and other things that they eat. They are planters, and they live on what they sow and harvest. The number of people and the land that they possess are large. They live like sheep without a shepherd because they do not have a king or lord obeyed by all, except for Your Highness at present. Each one is used to living and lives with his relatives, all together in one house. Until now, they have shown no sign of the errors of the gentiles[71] since they do not worship anything. Nonetheless, they used to eat the flesh of the enemies that they took and killed in war. They had their relatives as their wives, beginning with their sisters. All of them believed in dreams. They are hardworking men and very warlike. All this is in regard to the land and its people.

Once we arrived, all [the *indios*] came to serve us and brought us what they had for our sustenance. As Your Highness should agree, praise is due to the Maker of all things, visible and invisible, for what I will now tell Your Highness. The first year after we arrived here, so many locusts came to this land that they darkened the sun.[72] They blanketed the land and destroyed it, such that there was nothing green left in it. As a result, there was no gathering of food, or very little. Many natives of the land died. The majority of the Christian people who had come here returned to the port of Buenos Aires.

---

70. The feast of the Assumption is celebrated on August 15.
71. That is, pagans, in particular ancient Greeks and Romans. The errors of the gentiles were worshipping false gods and idols.
72. In the Book of Exodus, locusts are one of the plagues that afflicted Egypt; it was followed by the plague of darkness (Exod. 10).

A captain stayed in this port [of Asunción] with some Christians; I was one of those who stayed behind.

God who is infinite and whose mercy is infinite saved us from the dire straits we were in by putting in this river so many fish, and so big, that according to the natives of the land and to those of us who have lived here, such fish had never been seen before, nor have they been seen in this river since.[73] Such was the abundance that many of these natives lived off the Christians' leftovers. The snares in which these fish were caught were two fishing lines with many hooks. One of the fishermen who used them was a revered priest of the Order of Saint Jerome, and I was the other, because the people were occupied with clearing and sowing, and those who were sick guarded the town. And in this way, God sustained us until the crops were ripe for eating.

Through these labors, and other previous ones that I do not mention, I have never ceased working in the field of the Lord, administering the holy sacraments to the Christians in this holy church and in other places where I was with them. Likewise, [I have labored] in this land teaching these pagans the doctrine of God and reprehending them for their vices and bad habits, which were eating human flesh and having carnal intercourse with their relatives, and other bad habits, as I have said. I saw that God Our Lord had done us so many favors, and every day more, by giving us sustenance in the land. I also saw the growing desire for knowledge of the things of our Catholic faith that these pagan people demonstrated with their words. And I also saw that they were giving up their former vices (which were eating human flesh and others that I have mentioned). Thus, I decided to serve God and Your Highness in this way, because it is something that Your Highness urges the people who come to such lands to do.

I had no chance of informing Your Highness before undertaking the work so that I could perform it with the license and authority of Your Highness. Nevertheless, another priest and I proposed it to Captain Domingo de Irala, who ruled here at the time together with Your Highness's officials who resided here at the time. We told them how we wanted to sow the Word of God and his holy doctrine among

73. The anecdote evokes the story of how God provided the starving Israelites with bread from heaven (manna), which also appears in the Book of Exodus (Exod. 16).

these pagan peoples and work to bring them in to the fold and family of the holy mother church. They answered that they were very much in agreement and that Your Highness would be well served by this since, among other things, Your Highness had entrusted them with the conversion of the said *indios.*

In this spirit, which was mainly God's, another priest and I set out to do this work. We taught the *indios* how to cross themselves and the prayers of the holy mother church; we preached our holy Catholic faith and rebuked them for their vices, to wit, telling them not to eat human flesh, to stay away from the female relatives they had taken as wives, and to abstain from other vices that I have mentioned. This I told them through an interpreter who understood very well their language and ours; he is a son of Captain Gonzalo de Acosta, who is sailing there on this ship.[74] In this way I taught them and preached for a year and more, which is the time for catechism as established by law.[75]

The number of people who came to the doctrine was such that they did not fit in the church or in the square. There were old men and old women, people of every age, and mothers with their babes-in-arms. I saw the determination, ardor, and desire with which they came to the doctrine and how they had given up the vices that I had censured. They pestered me greatly to give them the water of baptism. Then there was the danger posed by a bad *indio* named Entigura, who had come to these *indios'* land from as far away as the coast of Brazil. He went around singing and telling those who followed him that he made Christians.[76] I told these *indios* that he was a scoundrel who lied and did not understand God's business; they agreed repeatedly that what I told them was true. Thus, after the time that I have mentioned, seeing their resolve in believing the creeds of our holy Catholic faith, I began giving them the water of holy baptism, without ceasing to instruct them in the holy doctrine to this day. They attend the teaching often and come to the church to hear

74. This was the same ship conveying Cabeza de Vaca back to Spain in the spring of 1545.

75. Catholic doctrine maintained that a true conversion could not be coerced. Therefore, adult converts had to receive religious instruction prior to baptism. To be considered truly effective, such instruction had to be conducted in a convert's native language.

76. In other words, that he could perform baptisms.

mass every Sunday and on holy days of obligation; they never leave without asking how many days they should work.[77]

I have told them that they should have but one woman, that they should receive her here in the church, and that the other women a man may have should be his servants to serve him and work in his fields. Therefore, many have asked to be married, but I have not wanted to marry them before informing Your Highness about it. The one exception is a *principal*, named Pedro de Mendoza,[78] who was with us from the outset and has been very good to all of us Christians in this land. He sent away the daughter of a *principal* that he had taken as his wife because she was a relative of a previous, deceased wife. Saying that he was a Christian and the he wanted to live as a Christian, he requested to be married to an unrelated woman he had. Consequently, I inquired among the *indios* whether she was his relative or whether there was any impediment that could prevent this marriage. The three proclamations were spoken in this church among the *indios* who came hither, admonishing them in their language to tell the truth. They all said that she was not his relative or the relative of any woman he had or had formerly had. And so I married them and put the veil on them. I have married none other since.

Many have refrained from asking for this sacrament of marriage because they have had children with some of their relatives, beginning with their sisters, and they know that I will not marry them. Let Your Highness decide what is to be done in these matters, whether we should marry them—given that they are now Christians—and whether an exception should be made for those who have children by their relatives, because separation feels harsh to them. Even though they say that they have nothing to do with these women, I know differently from some of their neighbors who tell me that they love their children very much and their mothers as well. This is the state of the doctrine up to now. Should Your Highness command me to continue what is begun, let Your Highness send me a supporting authorization so that no Christian or captain does anything in

77. Holy days of obligation are the days, other than Sundays, on which practicing Catholics are required to attend mass. The question refers to the number of days before the next obligatory mass.

78. It was common for native chieftains to take the name of their Spanish sponsor at baptism.

detriment of this holy doctrine. This much is in regard to the natives of the land.

In regard to the Christians, Your Highness should know that in spiritual matters they live like sheep without a shepherd because they know that there is no one here who has the power to compel them by means of censures.[79] They forgo confession and taking communion for two or three years. Some are openly living together with women of our nation and also with Christian *indias* born in the said land, having children by both the former and the latter, keeping them within their houses, under the pretext that I will now explain.

Lord, we found in this land a wicked custom, which is that the women are the ones who sow and harvest the food. Because the poverty of the soil would not allow us to sustain ourselves, each Christian was forced to take some of these local *indias*, whose relatives they appeased with trade items, to have them prepare their food. Having fallen into the hands of the Christians, they have had so many children by them that in this city there are five hundred or more children of Christians and Christian *indias* born in this land. Likewise, Lord, they have taken up the inherently bad habit of selling these *indias* to one another for trade items. I have reprimanded and continue to reprimand them for the former, especially, and for the latter. Let Your Highness decide what is best for the service of God in regard to the former and the latter. Likewise, Lord, some priests have come to this land as soldiers and, once here, they don religious garb and say mass. And since there is no one to hold them accountable, they do as they please, as Your Highness will hear from those traveling from here. Let Your Highness decide about it as needed. This is in regard to the mystical body of Christ.[80]

In regard to the real one, Your Highness should know that, for lack of diligence, we have no sacrament in this church even though it is such a necessary thing, especially in this land because of the big hurricanes that come hither and cause great damage, and all the more so for these *indios* when they come to the church to pray. Let Your Highness order that we be provided with sacrament, for everything

79. In Catholic cannon law, a censure is a penalty that involves limiting access to church services; it is intended to induce a change in behavior rather than as a punishment for bad deeds.

80. The Catholic Church, headed by Christ. Saint Paul talks about edifying the body of Christ in his letter to the Ephesians, 4:4–13.

may be gotten in this land except bread and wine. Likewise, let
Your Highness order that the church be covered with roof tile, for
there are people here to make it if they are paid for it. Likewise, two
Sevillian mass books,[81] and two sets of liturgical vestments, one for
the week and another one for Sundays and feast days, and a cope for
the processions,[82] and scored choir books for the sung masses that we
have here on saint days and Sundays,[83] because the church is very
lacking in all the service items I have mentioned.

Likewise, let Your Highness tell us the usage we should follow in
the service and the administration of the sacraments of the church
because in the beginning there were differences between some priests
regarding the usage we would follow. Having been reared in the holy
church of Seville, and knowing that the Sevillian usage was kept in
the Canary Islands and in Santo Domingo and in the other islands,
I maintained that we should follow that one, and thus it is followed
up until now. Let Your Highness decide what must be done about it.
Likewise, let Your Highness order that we clergymen who reside in
this province be very well treated, and supplied, and aided, and that
those who do not do what they should be punished, because there are
all kinds in this land. Some time ago, compelled by need, some who
have taken vows committed some excesses. Let Your Highness decide
what is most fitting for the service of God. Likewise, I beg Your Highness to order that no priest wishing to go to Spain be hindered, but
rather assisted and aided in everything needed to do so.

I have dared inform Your Highness about all the matters that I
have stated because I am the eldest resident in this land, and the first
to rule and govern the holy church of this city, having been in charge
of it for nearly seven years. I also did it because my conscience and
my zeal in the service of God and for the salvation of these souls
moved me to it. As God is my witness, it is true. And so that my wish
and purpose may be accomplished in this area, should Your Highness

81. In the early sixteenth century, the famous printer Jacobo Cromberger published elaborate and expensive mass books, or missals, in Seville. The missal contains
the prayers read, spoken, or sung during mass.

82. The garments that a Catholic priest wears during mass include a cassock,
a stole, and an alb. The cope is a long cloak called a *pluviale*, or raincoat, in Latin.

83. Necker (1979, 213) suggests that ornaments, processions, and singing height-
ened the missionaries' status among the Guaraní because they matched key elements
of shamanic performance.

not provide a bishop, grant me this charge and guardianship of the *indios* of this land, forty leagues into the surrounding territory, so that I may work in this land and this holy church as I always have. And as a means of support for myself, my family, and my house, grant me a third of the tithe of this holy church or whatever best serves Your Highness. And thus, I beg Your Highness to find out about everything that is written here in this letter from those who are on their way there and who have long resided in this land.

May our Lord keep and increase the very powerful person of Your Highness as your humble vassal wishes, from this city of Asunción on March 1, 1545.

> *Your Highness's humble vassal and chaplain,*
> *who kisses your royal hands and feet.*
> *Francisco de Andrada*

———————◆◆◆———————

Martín González to Emperor Charles V (June 25, 1556)

The letter written by Martín González, a cleric of unknown affiliation, adds to the epistolary stream of outrage at Domingo de Irala.[84] González wishes to inform Emperor Charles V about Irala's uninterrupted misdeeds after the imprisonment of Governor Álvar Nuñez Cabeza de Vaca. The cleric's denunciation centers on the scandalous mistreatment of indigenous women, which violated a number of colonial laws. Like other defenders of the natives, González uses hyperbole to underscore the savagery of the conquistadors and the meekness of the natives.[85] González also switches perspective in order to distance himself from the conquistadors' wrongs. When referring to the comings and goings of the expedition, he uses the first person plural "we," but when writing about violence being perpetrated he refers, perhaps with a measure of irony, to "the Christians" or "they."

84. Archivo Histórico Nacional, Colección Documentos de Indias, diversos-colecciones, 24, N.12.

85. The paradigmatic defender of the *indios* was Bartolomé de las Casas, whose incendiary rhetoric has been the source of much debate. See Keen (1969).

González's appeal to the crown, however, is not solely based on moral grounds. The case against the conquistadors had practical and even mercantile overtones: since the land and its people were so intricately intertwined, the destruction of one implied the devastation of the other. The Spaniards sought to conquer territory, but they also relied on the land's natives as providers of food, labor, and services, which included fighting on their side. Moreover, González portrays Irala's infamous dallying with the *indias* as a disservice to the crown because it distracts him from his dual mission of finding the Sierra de la Plata and supporting the evangelization of the natives.

Much like the conquistadors' ambivalent relationship with the natives, González's rhetoric reveals an ambivalent perspective on the native women whom he means to defend. Remarkably, he does not present them as passive objects. Rather, González recognizes the women's humanity and diverse identities as wives, mothers, daughters, sisters, and cousins. The indigenous family unit appears as a symbol of the natives' civility and reveals a certain degree of autonomy. But with another stroke of the pen, González turns the women into little more than discursive tropes to underscore the interrelated shortcomings of the Spaniards' religious and economic efforts. The conquistadors use the women's bodies for sexual pleasure, and González uses them as a pawn in the seemingly endless debates sparked by the departure of Governor Pedro de Mendoza. Nonetheless, González's text stands out as a welcome contrast to the one written by Domingo Martínez, for whom the natives differ only nominally from savages.

González's letter hints at a complicated reality that his Manichean worldview cannot register. In multiple instances, the representation of the natives as passive victims of incorrigible Spaniards gives way to evidence of indigenous agency. First, among the native peoples of the Río de la Plata, the exchange of women was a customary way to establish and cement allegiances. Therefore, despite the violence surely involved in many cases, the natives may have seen the union of their women with Spaniards in a more positive light than did González. In theory, these relationships obligated Spaniards to lend armed assistance to the families of the women they took. This may also imply that not all the raids against the natives were dictated by the conquistadors, but by their native allies according to their own agendas. Similarly, González denounces the fact that native women were buried according to the natives' barbaric practices, but this might indicate that it was, in fact, the natives who managed to maintain and even impose their traditional practices. The society of Spaniards and Guaraní in Paraguay was intimately intertwined at every level, perhaps more so than in other New World regions given the settlers' isolation. One of the results of the communion is that, whereas in most of Spanish America native languages are mostly spoken by ethnic minorities, Guaraní remains an official language understood by most Paraguayans.

In the midst of intrigue among potential leaders and their steady drive for the Sierra de la Plata, González's letter reminds us of the importance of considering the perspectives of the spiritual conquistadors who always played a role in the Spanish colonization of the New World. Though not devoid of certain biases, their narratives contrast with and complement those of the military conquistadors.

———————◆—————

Sacred Cesarean Catholic Royal Majesty,

We chaplains in this land are especially obliged to report to Your Majesty, and I in particular since I have taught the doctrine and baptized these your sheep. Therefore, seeing the damage and constant labors that they have suffered, and feeling their pain, through this my letter, I decided to inform Your Majesty of the events that took place in this land after the imprisonment of Álvar Núñez Cabeza de Vaca, who was Your Majesty's governor in this province. Moreover, through these unpolished verses, I decided to publish and tell about the great harm and constant labors that these poor people, Your Majesty's local-born subjects, have suffered and suffer. I beg Your Majesty to receive from me, your chaplain, this small service, together with my will and zeal for spreading and increasing our Holy Catholic Faith in the service of Our Lord and of Your Majesty.

You already know and have been informed about the imprisonment of Cabeza de Vaca who, besides being seized by Your Majesty's officials, was sent to prison by Captain Vergara, who now rules as governor of this land by Your Majesty's command.[86] I can assure

---

86. As in previous letters, Domingo de Irala is called Vergara after his birthplace. Irala officially assumed the governorship of the Río de la Plata in 1555.

Your Majesty that if Vergara had not provided his encouragement, favor, and help, the officials would not have had enough power to arrest Cabeza de Vaca. Even though Vergara was sick at the time, all the people in the land (or most of them) obeyed him because he had been in command for a long time. Thus, Vergara was able to do and to perpetrate what he did in disservice to Your Majesty, causing the destruction and loss of this land and its natives. The rebellious officials issued a proclamation to better implement and to achieve successfully what they had begun. They declared liberty, implying that Your Majesty's governor meant to subjugate them all, and claimed that what they did was done in the name of freedom. The officials spoke of subjection under Cabeza de Vaca, but I guarantee Your Majesty that afterward what we had was not just subjection but total destruction of everyone, except for the officials' friends and allies, who were content and acted as lords. The governor was put behind bars, and the justices he appointed were imprisoned and shamefully shorn of their beards, as Your Majesty will be more fully and better informed by those who go there in your service. It is now clear that this was done so that the officials could rule, returning the said Captain Vergara to his former authority and exhausting and destroying this land, as they all have done.

Through deceit, the officials brought many people to their side to better implement and achieve their aims. They accomplished this because some were, as they were, sick, and some were in the company of others who were wounded and were set in favor of Captain Vergara and Your Majesty's officials. In short, all were miserable. The worst and most harmful thing was that the people were new in the land and they could not survive without the goodwill of those who were here;[87] therefore, by force, by choice, or by need, the officials brought each one to the side they had embraced. And it was not only the people's need. They also claimed that Your Majesty's governor wanted to usurp this land from Your Majesty, which they supported by saying that he had taken down the royal banner from a ship and that he had ordered one of his own to be flown. They also alleged other things that, because they are prolix and have little foundation,

87. The new people, those who came with Cabeza de Vaca, depended for survival on the *conquistadores viejos*, who remained from the Pedro de Mendoza expedition, for their knowledge and experience of the land.

I will not mention. Nonetheless, it seems to me, according to what I feel and understand, and what I have seen with my own eyes, that their falsehood and deviousness raised these charges to win over the poor people so they could accomplish and avenge their passion.

Having imprisoned the governor, the officials determined to destroy the land in order to satisfy their friends and supporters. To keep them loyal in any situation that might arise due to these actions, the officials gave many licenses to those who favored them so they might roam the land. And the latter were such that I can certify to Your Majesty that, like fire, they burned and ravaged the land wherever they went. They took the *indios'* women, daughters, sisters, and relatives; if they happened to be new mothers with babies at their breasts, they left the babies and threw them on the ground, and they took and brought the mothers with them. Some did not want to give up their women, but by force and against their will, threatened, and some nearly killed, they gave them up in order to avoid death, even though they suffered much toil and loneliness without them. Out of fear, the *indios* had hidden their women in the woods, from where they had to bring them out. And if some *indios* were lazy or tardy in carrying out orders, these ravagers unleashed their anger on them, stabbing and clubbing them, and otherwise mistreating them, taking away their houses and all that they had in them.

These *indios* were so mistreated by those who commanded, as well as by their friends and supporters, that they decided to kill some Christians. And so they killed two or three Christians who were camping among them. This they did because they felt as injured as they were: night or day, they never had a moment of peace. Rather, they had to stay watchful and vigilant to guard their daughters and women. The women never came home or performed their duty of preparing meals and taking care of the children because Christians roamed the land. The land was in an uproar due to the death of the Christians. So, in order to better achieve their aim of attacking the *indios*, the Christians convoked and called two *indio* nations called Guatatas y Apiraes, who are very volatile and were the enemies of the Carios. Once these *indios* and Christians had joined forces, the Carios, who saw their enemies gathered against them, decided to rise up in such a way that few, if any, were left who did not rise up, openly or in secret. With the land in an uproar, two hundred Christians with two thousand of the aforementioned *indios* went out to attack them. In many skirmishes that they had with the Carios, they killed a great number of them and, as a sign of vengeance, chopped off their heads, which the Christians' *indio* allies took to their land. They would not have done or even dared to do any of this were it not for the support of the Christians.

Due to these wars, seeing the great damage that the Christians and their allies caused—burning their houses, and razing and destroying their crops—and seeing that they could not escape should the war in this land continue any longer, many of the Carios lost it by leaving, while others came to surrender, which was granted. And so it happened. These poor people have always been and are peaceful, though desolate because of their great suffering and loss, losing their sons, daughters, and women, and suffering hunger due to the razing of their crops, as I have said.

The Carios returned to their home and began to rebuild their houses, which were all burned down, and to tend to their lands and crops. Due to the war and the fear of the Christians' *indio* allies, for days they did not dare to come out of the forest, where they and their children suffered hardships because they had little food, only thistles and small game that they caught in the woods. They spent many days like this, and because of their want, many children young and old were lost.

No sooner were the Carios in their houses and settlements than the friends and supporters of Captain Vergara and the officials and captains roamed the land again. Not satisfied with the damages that these *indios* had suffered, the captain sent some interpreters among them with orders to bring *indias*, not only for himself but also for whomever he wanted. In this way, they again pursued and destroyed the *indios*, worse than before, so that many of them were laden with children. Seeing themselves so mistreated, they died from sheer grief, not only the father but also the children who, being very young, fell into the fires and, having no mothers, burned there because no one took them out. Without someone to feed them, other children resorted to eating dirt, and so they died. Others who were very young and at their mothers' breasts when they were taken away stayed there on the ground; some old women took some of them and squeezed their breasts until they produced milk. And so they raised them thin, sickly, and wretched. Thus, because the children could not get enough, their days came to an end.

About these *indias* that the interpreters brought, Your Majesty should know that they were shared with Captain Vergara, because if those who were not his friends or supporters did not give him half, they could not keep any, for this is how he dealt with those who were of contrary opinion. And whenever he took women away, he did not return any of them to the *indios*, even though they came looking for them, because he always found a way to keep the women for himself or for his friends and supporters. Seeing that they were not given back, the *indios* kept crying all the way to their land and in their homes. Knowing that they remained in the hands of the Christians, the mothers, aunts, and relatives cried night and day. There was so much crying that from sheer heartache and not eating, both the men and women ended up dying.

Many of the *indias* who remained with the Christians found themselves so harassed that they fled to their lands, but they were brought back and then whipped and abused. Other women, harried and wishing to see their children and husbands, and seeing that they could not go to them, hanged themselves. Those who did not do this gorged themselves with dirt because they would rather kill themselves than suffer the life that many Christians gave them. Other women were kept so locked up that not even the sun could see them. If the Christians who kept them saw anything that they did not like, even when it was not as it seemed, they killed or burned them out of jealousy. And such was the dissolution in this land.

To tell and tally in this letter the number of *indias* that have been brought to this city since governor Cabeza de Vaca was jailed would be without end. But it seems to me that there must be about fifty thousand *indias*, probably more than less.[88] Now, at present, there must be among the Christians fifteen thousand, and all the rest are dead. They die from mistreatment and abuse. Given that the Christians are the cause of their deaths, they should bury them in churches or graveyards. This they do not do. Instead, they bury them and have them buried in the fields, as is the custom of the *indios*.

If I tried to tell in this letter about their mistreatment, it seems to me that I would never finish, but I will say that there are some who make the poor people dig all day in their lands and fields, walking

---

88. Though these numbers are unreliable as empirical data, the deeper truth of widespread abuse remains.

over them and sowing large crops to be able to sell them. And this would be good, if the poor people ate and rested at night. On the contrary, they do not eat unless it is some sad pittance they bring from the fields, and they spend most of the night spinning to dress the lord who owns them and to make enough for him to sell. As if the labors and constant toils that the *indios* had—in the fields as well as in building adobe houses to sell and other chores—were not enough, a greater burden has now come upon them: grinding sweet cane to make molasses, which is not only drunk and eaten but even sold. Now it is treated as a commodity.

It is impossible to try to count and number the *indias* that each Christian has presently, but it seems to me that there are those who have eighty and a hundred *indias*, among which it is impossible that there are not mothers and daughters, sisters and cousins.[89] It seems obvious that whoever does not have ins and outs with them must have great moral fortitude because the opportunity and circumstance are so ample at present that, as I say, only a saintly person would fail to fall into these dealings. In this matter, I can attest to Your Majesty that the *indios* have taken the worst possible example, because everything that the Spaniards do in secret with the *indias* is done openly among the *indios*, and then they come to tell me about it.

This notwithstanding, Your Majesty, what has scared me the most is seeing, as I have, the sale of free individuals as if they were captives. And so it happens that local-born free *indias* are sold for horses, dogs, and other things; thus, they are used like coin in the realms of Spain.[90] Not only this; it is known that an *india* was gambled away (I say one though there are many). This one had the misfortune of holding the candlestick and the light while they played for her; after she had been won, they undressed her and, without clothes, sent her with the man who won her, because the man who lost her said he had not gambled the dress she was wearing. This was sometimes done in the presence of the commander, who happened, on occasion, to make such a deal to appease everybody and to avoid discord. Nothing

89. The taboo against engaging in sexual relations with women of the same family is Biblical. The Book of Leviticus warns that "if there is a man who marries a woman and her mother, it is immorality; both he and they shall be burned with fire, so that there will be no immorality in your midst" (Lev. 20:14).

90. New World natives were officially regarded as Spanish subjects. Though they were subject to tribute, legally they could not be enslaved unless they were cannibals.

stopped the Christians from giving *indias*, as they did, as dowry when they gave their daughters in marriage. Likewise, at the time of their deaths, they paid debts they owed with the said *indias*. Moreover, they leave them to their children, and so the *indias* die.

These and other things have taken place in this land up until now, and besides this, I will tell Your Majesty that when the governor was imprisoned, some went against Your Majesty's officials. For this reason they have been pursued, apprehended, and mistreated,[91] and have even been called loyal by way of insult.

After Governor Cabeza de Vaca had departed, there was news that Christians—those who set out from Peru with Francisco de Mendoza—were coming by way of the Tinbues.[92] When Captain Vergara and his officers found this out, they wanted to leave the land. There were some scuffles and difficulties about this departure between Captain Vergara and some of the officers. The loyalists took this opportunity to approach the *contador*,[93] who was of the opinion that they should not leave the land until they found out who these people were. And so things reached a point where it seemed that all would be lost. Seeing the possible loss that could result, it was resolved that the only thing to do was for the *contador* to go find out who the said people were. Those who call themselves loyalists went with him.

When they returned, having seen that the Christians were those who had come with Mendoza, it was decided that up to two hundred fifty men would go to meet them. I joined this journey so as to better inform Your Majesty about whatever might happen in the land.

Making our way upriver, after ninety leagues, we left the ships and fifty men in a town, from where we proceeded inland. Forty leagues from the said town, we found a nation of *indios* who are called Mayas [Mbaya]. These fled at first for the great fear that they had due to their previous encounters with Christians. Afterward, the

91. González uses the verb "afianzar" which, according to the 1726 *Diccionario de autoridades*, could mean "to place a person on the rack."

92. In 1543, Diego de Rojas set out from Peru to explore the Tucumán region, which lies between Chile and the Río de la Plata. Rojas was killed and Francisco de Mendoza assumed command of the expedition. Mendoza managed to reach the ruins of Sancti Spíritus, where he found Irala's letter to those who might travel upriver. Mendoza decided to go to Asunción, but his men were against it. They killed Mendoza and went back to Peru.

93. Felipe de Cáceres.

indios sent certain messengers, who were not treated as they should have been. Seeing that the Christians would not come and given what they were asking for, the *indios* thought it better to burn their houses and leave. And so they slipped away without hurting any Christians.

Once these Maya *indios* had abandoned their settlements, as I have just told, Captain Vergara, seeing that they had left, gave the order to attack them. And so it was done with the assistance of local-born Cario *indios* who had gone with us and who may have numbered up to two or three thousand warriors. These Cario *indios* who went to war attacked many villages of the Mayas and those of other nearby nations. After the attack, they killed and seized so many *indios* that I do not know how to convey it in this letter. But I will say that it was a great pity to see the children and the old men and women dead, for the Carios only brought young men and women as presents for their lords. The persecution was not just in the towns and houses; they even searched the surrounding countryside to pursue them.

After this war, taking many of these Maya *indios* as prisoners and guides, Captain Vergara moved on until he reached a small river. Once at the river, his guides lost their way because they had not been through there in many days. Having lost the way and seeing that the *indios* could not find it, he had one of the guides burned, and two others were killed. From here, we turned onto another route, where we came upon some villages of the Chanes, among whom the Christians caused much death and destruction.

Not content with this, Captain Vergara sent a captain called Nuflo de Chaves[94] to take some men to attack a village that lay ahead. In the morning, Chaves went and attacked the village. They captured a number of *indios* and killed a great many people, including children, men, and the elderly.

After this war, we proceeded, destroying and killing anyone the Christians met. When it was not the Christians, the *indios* that they had taken in their service did the killing, and the Christians allowed

---

94. Nuflo or Nufrio de Chávez (1518–68) reached the Río de la Plata along with Cabeza de Vaca. In 1548, Chávez traveled to Lima on behalf of Domingo de Irala to settle the matter of territorial jurisdiction. Later, in 1561, Chávez founded Santa Cruz de la Sierra not far from the city of the same name in present-day Bolivia.

it and approved of it. Wherever they went, the *indios* brought them prisoners; they caused great misery in capturing them, by taking everything they had and burning down their houses and taking away their provisions.

In this way we went up to the Moyganos.[95] No *indios* would wait for us in their towns because those who chose to wait and came to bring us food were taken, seized, tied up, and forced to guide the Christians to the villages where they wanted to go. And when one mistook the way for not having gone by there in many days, Captain Vergara ordered that pieces of his flesh be ripped off with pliers; and so the poor *indio* ended his days.

When we reached the Moyganos, as I have said, the local *indios* welcomed us because they were reassured by Captain Garci Rodríguez, who was leading the vanguard. Once we arrived, the *indios* gave us many things, such as food and other things they had brought. Seeing that the commander distributed them among his friends and companions, the rest of the people were grieved; they demanded to have a *procurador*. Thus, Captain Camargo was named and elected to serve in this land and before Your Majesty.

Having done this, the commander decided to attack the Miaracano *indios*, who were near these *indios* with whom we were staying. The Miaracanos were not doing any evil or harm to the latter. In this war the Christians killed and seized a great many people, and all the remaining enemy *indios* were destroyed. The Christians did not take any of these *indios* except for the young men and women, for the rest were killed by their *indio* allies. From here we advanced, making war on many villages and houses, as I have already said, until we reached the Mogranoes, who, knowing what had happened and fearing that the same would happen to them, awaited us ready for war. As soon as we entered their village, they started shooting their weapons at us, killing some Christians. Then the Christians and their horses charged so that the Mogranoes quickly left the town, and the Christians seized many women. We stayed fifteen days in this village.

A few days later, while in the village of the defeated Mogranoes, one of the Carios was wounded while searching for food. Thus, the Mogranoes were labeled as slaves and attacked. During the attack the

95. Since indigenous communities in the Río de la Plata were often identified by the name of their leader, the different groups that González mentions do not necessarily represent distinct ethnicities.

Christians killed many people, including children, old women, and warriors, a total sum of more than four thousand souls; they took more than two thousand *indios*, whom they brought as slaves. Your Majesty's officials and the captain withheld the royal fifth, but they did not think it was necessary to brand them.

From here we departed and went to the Cimeonos because we had heard that some of the Christians who had gone with Juan de Ayolas were there. Once we arrived, we asked about them. The Cimeonos said that the Christians had been killed by their enemies when they had gone to war against them. For this reason, the Christians imprisoned the leader of these *indios* and one of his sons, who had come to them in peace, treated them well, and brought them food.

From here we went to the Corocotoques, taking the aforementioned prisoners. This caused upheaval throughout the land because the *indios* saw and knew that even though the leader and his son had come in peace and brought food, they had been seized and taken. Having gathered information from the aforementioned *indios*, we left from there toward the Tamacocíes, because they said there was white metal there and that, on the right-hand side as we went, there was yellow metal. And it was agreed that we should go to the Tamacocíes. When we arrived, they came in peace, being, as they were, *indios* that had served and dealt with Christians. There we were informed about Peru. Knowing how close we were to the kingdoms of Peru, it was agreed by the captain and Your Majesty's officials to send Captain Nuflo de Chaves and others to Peru. The rest of the people returned by way of the Corocotoques. Here there was disagreement between Your Majesty's officials and the captain about the mission. The captain wanted to go to Peru after Captain Nuflo de Chaves. But it happened that all the people sided with the officials and prevented him from going to Peru. Because of this and owing to the demands that they made on him, he was forced to resign his command. Captain Gonzalo de Mendoza[96] was elected as commander until we reached the Paraguay and this city of Asunción. Among these Corocotoques, great wars were waged, where the Christians killed countless children and many other people; many also were seized.

We left from here, bringing these captives, along with all those who were seized as prisoners and slaves in the wars the Christians waged along the way, until they reached the port of San Fernando.

96. See note 27 in Domingo de Irala's letter.

As soon as Captain Vergara arrived in the village that had been settled when we left, he found out how Captain Diego de Abrego had been elected as commander [in Asunción]. Since they had never seen eye to eye, Captain Vergara, in collusion with some individuals who were there, told the people that Captain Diego de Abrego had taken away all their property and *indios*, and that he had distributed them to whomever he wanted. This caused such uproar among the people that they chose to follow Captain Vergara. And so he came to this city with weapons in hand; entering by night, he proclaimed that anybody who left their house that night would be regarded as a traitor and would forfeit their life and property.

The next day Captain Diego de Abrego went with his scribe on behalf of Your Majesty to demand the assistance of Captain Vergara and Your Majesty's officials in keeping the land quiet, peaceful, and serene. All of this was recorded by Captain Diego de Abrego's scribe, who also recorded the things they said in reply. Then, after three or four days, they seized the said Captain Diego de Abrego and held him prisoner, burdening him with chains, until he freed himself and escaped from the jail.

Once Captain de Abrego left, some of his friends joined him and decided to go by way of San Vicente[97] to the kingdoms of Spain in order to inform Your Majesty about what had happened in this land. When Captain Vergara found out, he pursued them with people on foot and on horseback. They seized them and brought them, shamefully handcuffed; some were wounded. Captain de Abrego was imprisoned again. Tired of being in jail, he decided to escape, and so he did. He left, taking with him a relative of his who was also in jail. After leaving, he went into the woods, where he wandered for four years. After this, Captain de Abrego was seized again.

At that time, Captain Vergara sent people throughout the land who disturbed and destroyed it. The Christians took the *indios'* wives and daughters and all that they had; they burned their houses and snatched their supplies, and caused them great harm, because the *indios* did not want to give up their wives and daughters. Seeing the harm that came to the natives and the conquistadors because of these raids, and that some got all the benefit while some who backed them never profited from them, the general *procurador* of the province

---

97. See note 57 in Juan Pavón's letter.

decided to confront Captain Vergara. When the captain heard about his intentions, he sent word for him not to confront him because he would have him hanged if he did. And so the *procurador* decided to remain silent. When the conquistadors heard about this, Miguel de Rutre in particular asked the *procurador* why he did not do his duty on behalf of the land and its conquistadors, as he had sworn. Given that the *procurador* would not do it for fear of Captain Vergara, Miguel de Rutre said, "I will confront him and I will make him comply or desist." Captain Vergara, who was about twenty leagues from here, heard about all of this and quickly returned. Once here, he went as a friend to see the *procurador* but had him arrested and placed under heavy guard. Miguel de Rutre found out and went to talk to the captain about the fact that the *procurador* was blameless. As soon as he arrived, Rutre was seized and imprisoned. That night, Captain Vergara had them garroted without confession, saying that they did not need to confess, even though they asked for it many times and he had priests in his house.

After Miguel de Rutre's and Camargo's execution, those who had been sent to survey the land so that it could be distributed returned. Captain Vergara found trifling reasons not to distribute the land, but this did not stop him from sending his interpreters to bring back everything they found there, including *indios* and women, as they had before. Then, Captain Vergara decided to make an *entrada*. Against the will of the majority, he left the *contador* Felipe de Cáceres in charge. Captain Diego de Abrego, who was in the wilderness and had always shown himself loyal to Your Majesty, saw many of his people leave to avoid being prosecuted and disarmed (as all of them have always been since Governor Cabeza de Vaca's imprisonment); he came out to round them up and gathered them in a thicket. When Captain Vergara, who now rules as governor, returned, he fell upon de Abrego with eight hundred souls, or rather more, of local and neighboring *indios* and Christians, many of whom had been pressed into his service under great duress. He routed Captain de Abrego and seized three Christians, whom he later sentenced to be hanged, and so they were. Others who were apprehended afterward were taken to the gallows, but they pleaded and were spared. However, he assuaged his fury by taking everything they had to offset all his costs and expenses. He even killed a *principal* from this land, alleging that he had fed Captain Diego de Abrego and his men.

Having done this, Captain Vergara decided to continue his journey, and so he did, leaving the *contador* in command, as he had done before. Captain Vergara threatened the *contador* into swearing that he would carry out the *provisiones* he had made, by which most or all of those who had been with Diego de Abrego were destroyed. Not satisfied with this, he gave permission to kill Captain Diego de Abrego, who was found one night in a thicket, blinded by sickness and alone. They drove a crossbow bolt through his heart, from which he died without uttering a word or calling to God.

After Captain Diego de Abrego was killed, Captain Vergara returned from the journey he had undertaken. Because he was trying to prevent Garci Rodríguez from crossing over to the kingdoms of Peru, he had not taken the road he should have, and the land he found was deserted. (Rodríguez intended to go inform Your Majesty about what had taken place in the land.) As he made his way back, two thousand *indios* born in this land died of hunger, cold, and mistreatment. Having returned, he did not forget his bad habit of harassing and taking the *indias* from the *indios,* for himself as well as to give to others who had gone with him. What is more, before leaving on the *entrada,* he had given the Christians much license to roam and rob the land, under the guise that his exploration of the land was in the service of Your Majesty.

Next, Captain Vergara wanted once again to undertake his *entrada,* notwithstanding the fact that earlier he had killed many people and hung many old women in the province of the Paraná because they were greedy in giving up their daughters. For this reason, the *indios* hid everything they had and stayed alone in their homes. Seeing them without women, the Christians claimed that the *indios* were rebellious and at war; and so they killed them and looked for the *indias* in the woods. Others gave the *indias* out of fear. In this way, they brought many of them, some of whom Captain Vergara gave to some people to oblige them to go with him whenever he went on the *entrada.*

After all this, news came about how Your Highness was making Captain Vergara governor of this province; the knowledge of this caused him to desist from pursuing the *entrada.* Captain Vergara then sent Captain Nuflo de Chaves with certain people to look for and find Bartolomé Justiniano, who was bringing the *provisión.* While on his way, Captain Chaves abandoned the task to attack some *indios* because he heard no one had reached them yet. He fought with them, killing and seizing many young men and women, whom he distributed among all those who were with him. While Captain Nuflo de Chaves was thus engaged, Bartolomé Justiniano came and reached this city of Asunción. He delivered the *provisión* that he had, which he presented, and once presented, Captain Vergara was obeyed, as Your Highness commanded in your *provisión*. Once the *provisión* arrived and was obeyed, Captain Vergara ordered a census of the land. After the census was taken and the results were brought, he distributed the land among his friends and foreign supporters and people who had recently come from Peru and other places.

With the land in this state, Captain Vergara decided to go again to the Paraná. As he was leaving, the bishop[98] and Martín de Vicente arrived in this city with certain *provisiones* from Your Majesty, some of which were read. Before the arrival of the bishop and the distribution of the land, Captain Vergara never ceased to skin the land's natives and to take away their daughters and women. Not content with this, he allowed the neighbors of San Vicente to remove *indias* from this land and to take them to San Vicente, and so they took many. These, most victorious prince and lord, are only some of the things that have happened in this land so long as Your Majesty's justice has been lacking herein. Through my sacrifices I pray the Lord that he will move Your Majesty to always provide us with your justice so that through it we may serve Our Lord God and Your Majesty. May Our Lord keep the Your Majesty's victorious person and greatly increase your years, according to the wishes of your loyal vassals, so that you may keep us in peace and justice. From this city of Asunción, on the twenty-fifth of June of 1556.

Holy Cesarean Catholic Royal Majesty, the humble chaplain of Your Majesty who kisses your royal hands and feet,
Martín González

---

98. Bishop Pedro de la Torre, who arrived in Asunción in March 1556. His notorious greed led him to disregard a royal decree that prohibited territorial expansion, allowing only the settlement of lands already conquered. Instead, the bishop supported Irala in further exploration and conquest.

Domingo Martínez to Emperor Charles V (July 2, 1556)

A member of the original expedition of Pedro de Mendoza, Domingo Martínez obtained an *encomienda* of *indios* in recompense for his services but risked losing them when he decided to become ordained as a priest. Martínez acknowledges that clerics were not permitted to own *indios*. However, he artfully attempts to circumvent the law's enforcement by (a) enumerating exhaustively his meritorious service to the crown, and (b) attempting to take advantage of a dubious loophole by pointing out that the *indios* were given to him as a conquistador, not as a cleric. Looking ahead, he requests that he be able to leave them to his illegitimate *mestiza* daughters.[99]

In theory, the legal rights of *mestizos* were limited, not only because of their mixed stock but because they were generally the product of informal, and therefore illegitimate, unions between conquistadors and native women. This explains Martínez's efforts to justify why his daughters should inherit his *encomienda*. His lengthy discussion of the dangers faced not only by his own brood but by *mestizas* in general positions women at the heart of the battle between civilization and barbarism. *Mestizas* must be raised as Christians, endowed, and properly married to Spaniards; they must be kept away at all costs from the bestial *indios* so that they do not regress into savagery. This letter paints a very different portrait of the natives from those offered by the clerics Francisco de Andrada and Martín González. For Martínez, the natives are neither pure souls nor meek victims. On the contrary, he speaks plainly in deeming that the *indios*' baseness was worthy of torture and execution. In his account, the conquistadors and their offspring are always under threat of the *indios*, whom he presents as lazy, conniving, uncivilized, and ultimately useless. Barring cynicism, Martinez's contentions are paradoxical as his letter also makes clear the importance of native men and women to the success of the colony.

On the other hand, the various services to the crown that Martínez itemizes are quite revealing of the quotidian details of the conquest. Though all the conquistadors were adventurous, not all were necessarily proficient in any trade that would advance the enterprise. A supplementary amount of ingenuity was needed for

---

99. Archivo Histórico Nacional, Colección Documentos de Indias, diversos-colecciones, 24, N.19.

these adventurers to survive on their own, deprived of the tools and technologies that were common in Europe. Thus, Martínez's boasting about the seemingly trivial—but actually crucial—work of making fishhooks, needles, or combs is not unjustified. The lack of fishhooks, needles for mending clothes, and combs for personal hygiene could each have potentially disastrous consequences, just as the absence of a dagger when encountering an *indio*. Martínez notes that all his inventions had contributed to the base requirements of conquistadors. Moreover, he insists that they were very profitable all around.

The text written by Domingo Martínez presents significant contrasts, in both form and content, with the letters produced by captains such as Irala, officials such as Pavón, and clerics such as González. Martínez, the student-turned-tradesman, does not show much interest in the political, legal, or spiritual matters that do not trouble him directly. Moreover, Martínez borders on irreverence when, instead of humbly requesting a boon, he admonishes the emperor to fulfill his just and Christian duty toward such entrepreneurial conquistadors as himself.

———————◆•◆•◆———————

Holy Caesarean Catholic Majesty,

The father has a responsibility to his children, and the king and prince to his vassals and servants. The father takes special care of his children, just as the lord takes care of his servants, and the prince and king of his vassals, providing and remedying their needs, rewarding those who do in their service what is just and proper, granting them favors, as well as withholding them according to how well or poorly they have obeyed and been loyal to their father or lord or king. Considering this, I dare recount to Your Holy Majesty the service that for my part I have rendered in this province to Your Catholic Majesty— as a true servant and at a time when this province was in such great need, as Your Majesty knows and will plainly see.

First, when Buenos Aires was first settled, given that I had come from Spain with Your Catholic Majesty's governor, Don Pedro de Mendoza, and that I was a poor student without any knowledge of a trade, and seeing the need there was at the time, I made fishhooks. They were among the first to be made, which to this day has yielded and yields great benefit, because without them trading with the *indios* would be unfeasible, as well as fishing, especially since, at that time, it was our only livelihood. Afterward, having come to this city of Our Lady of Asunción, I made fishhooks. Likewise, I made combs as well. Whereas now there are many who make them, this was at a time when men could not find a comb to comb their beards, and they are a necessity in this land. After this, I made knives for trading, polished and hafted like the ones brought from Flanders, to trade with the *indios*, wherein nothing has been lost, but rather it has been very profitable. Besides this, there is great need of small fishhooks (as thick as thick needles, and thinner), and hammering them out is too much work. Because a great many are needed, though I had never seen casts or how they were used, with the help of God, who grants his favors to those who undertake a virtuous task, I made a gadget which, likewise, has been and remains very useful still. Many do this now, and it is all necessary because whatever is needed elsewhere is taken from here. Likewise, I have made bellows, like a silversmith's, which have been necessary. I have also made cutting knives and scissors for the women and *mestizas* (of which, praise God, there are plenty), as well as sewing and embroidering needles, for the officers as much as for the women and *mestizas*, in large quantities. And I have made large needles for making sandals and needles, and moreover, daggers, which have been necessary and still are, because there are many who have found themselves faced with *indios* and, for lack of a dagger, the *indios* defy them and do with them what they will. These daggers have been, as everyone says, as good as or even better than some that come from the kingdoms of Spain. I have made other things, mostly trifles, which would be too long to describe.

Besides this, and the most useful thus far, was a small screw press I made because sweet cane for sugar was planted, and we had nothing suitable for pressing it. It had been pressed with some wedges, but, as later experiments revealed, one-fourth, at least, was lost. This screw press was the first to be made. Later I made others that were better, which has garnered great benefit in the land and still does. I wanted to make and have made a wooden wheel, large and very heavy, for milling the cane. There is very great need for such a wheel, because the cane is currently milled by force of arms, in the way and manner that it is milled in Motril[100] and like the olives and

---

100. A town in the southern Spanish province of Granada; historically famous as an enclave of sugarcane growing in Europe.

sumac[101] are milled. Since I do not know how well it will work until I test it, I say no more.

It seems to me that in these things I have rendered exceptional service to Your Holy Catholic Majesty (not to mention the common work and general service that I have provided in this conquest like anyone else, with my effort and arms, at my cost and initiative, without having been excluded from any task that came up). Taking into account the aforementioned things (for which I give many an infinite thanks to Our Lord Jesus Christ who has seen fit to grant me the grace and skill to serve Him by helping others and serving Your Catholic Majesty), should Your Majesty deem that what I have mentioned above in any way may be regarded as services that merit some reward (especially having been done at a time of great need), I beg Your Majesty, as a humble servant and vassal (which I regard myself to be and am), that Your Holy Majesty may grant me the few *indios* that Governor Domingo de Irala, in Your Catholic Majesty's name, has given and entrusted to me, so that they may serve me as they do the rest. Moreover, let Your Majesty grant that they be for my illegitimate children. If this were not possible (since they are not legitimate), to prevent the land from falling into the hands of *mestizos* and locals (for reasons that Your Majesty can plainly see), I ask that they may be bestowed on a Christian who would marry one of my daughters in this land. In this way, I believe that it will be possible to prevent many calamities, because the Christian will have charge of his wife and of all her brothers and sisters. Thus, it will not be as they say it is in New Spain and the kingdoms of Peru, where those who know say that the *mestizas* are in the hands of the *indios*, isolated and unable to protect themselves. Such a situation is very harmful, not only because their bodies are tainted, which is the least of the matter, but also because their souls are lost. For they engage, as they do, with beasts that are without reason or good example, disorderly in their vices, and incorrigible. Thus, they must do as the *indios*, and they do not live as Christians, and they die without knowing God. This is very painful for one who has served Your Catholic Majesty

---

101. The sumac (*Rhus coriaria*) fruit, dried and ground, is used as a spice and for pickling olives; the bark and the leaves, which contain tannic acid, are used in leather tanning. The plant spread throughout Spain after the Arab conquest of the Iberian Peninsula in the eighth century.

for so long, without having received anything useful to meet one's needs and to provide for one's children so that they may remain among Catholics and be instructed in the faith, even if by force. In these parts, nobody takes pity on those who have nothing. Therefore, may Your Catholic Caesarean Majesty concern himself with such consequential neglect: evangelization was so dear to the Creator of the world, for he died to save us. It might seem ungrateful not to follow the example that He left on earth.

Consider, Your Holy Majesty, what a pitiful and painful thing it is that a father who served twenty-something years without any reward whatsoever, neither given to him nor gained in the land, now, at the time of his death, knows that his children will fall into the hands of the *indios*. More so such uncivilized *indios* as these: they would not even prepare food for themselves but for the help of the Christians, who give them the tools with which they cook their very meager portions. Thus, those who are removed from contact with Christians, who cannot succor them, die like beasts. Though a father see his son, or the son his father, on the brink of death, the most they do is put a little water in a gourd and a little flour in another, and make a little fire, and they are more than satisfied.

Vices and evil deeds are so common and frequent among them that it is almost too much to tell. Any admonition they receive, they seem willing to follow, but the action comes late or never. Even though some of them have been baptized for so long now, coming here for mass on feast days, they are so gullible that if an old woman or an *indio*—the least fortunate among them—stands up claiming to be God, or that they are not baptized unless he baptizes them, the whole land empties when they leave to be baptized again or to hear his word as if it were God's. Just a few days ago it was necessary to execute some of them, which is the only way to stop this. The *indias* who have been among us for eighteen years are very crafty and astute, conning the Christian into trusting them so that they do not watch them. As Your Catholic Majesty knows, they cannot be trusted to spin even an ounce of cotton, except by weight, because they will burn it, hide it, or give it away. They rejoice only in ruining the Christians and destroying all there is, without rhyme or reason. When they are asked about it, they reply, "*Erua*," which is to say, "I do not know"; even if they know why, once they say no, it is useless to try to get anything else out of them, even if you skin them. Even when they are going out to weed, it is necessary to go with them. Everything should be kept under lock and key. If they must spin, let it be by weighing the raw cotton and then the thread. The result at the end of the year is such that no one—from the governor to the least person—can support or pay the wages of a servant to work his *hacienda*. Rather, he must work it himself if he is to survive. This is all because of the *indios* when left to their own devices. Regarding the provisions, though there is corn year-round in the fields, it is necessary to be vigilant about sowing all the time, because the corn gets full of weevils after three months, or half a year at most, and it is a lot if it ever makes it to a year. So it happens that, if what is sown is lost, there is dearth. Of these things there is so much to tell that it is impossible to say it all.

There is plenty of proof of the wealth that has been gathered. And if we have not looked for more, let Your Sacred Majesty not blame the poor, innocent companions, obedient and humble subjects who do whatever those who govern want, humbly lowering their heads to do everything that is commanded in Your Catholic Majesty's name. May Your Catholic Majesty know that I am a man of fifty years, perhaps less but not more, and I want to dedicate what life I have left to the service of God. I need Your Catholic Majesty's help with this matter because I want to become a cleric. God in his clemency has seen fit that by order of Your Sacred Majesty a bishop has come to this land to ordain priests.[102] My ordination will serve God because I will serve Your Catholic Majesty better as a cleric than I would as a layperson. Because the land is as miserable as can be, I need favor and help in everything. If I am worthy, Your Sacred Majesty's endorsement will allow me to receive some alms from the church to help me in my need.

I thought it best not to overlook a scandal that has taken place in this land regarding a *provisión* from Your Catholic Majesty, which commands that the officials charge the tithe as it is done in the Spanish Indies, Cuba, Jamaica, and Santo Domingo. Everyone, including the clerics, thought that Your Catholic Majesty had commanded that the tithe be charged differently here than it is in the kingdoms of Spain. Since the tithe had not been paid as it is in Spain, when the bishop arrived, he extended public excommunications and censures,

102. See note 98 in Martín González's letter.

causing great scandal. This has been regarded as poorly done, because he does not have proper documentation, though this should have been recorded at the Casa de Contratación,[103] as your Catholic Majesty decrees in one of your *provisiones*. Let Your Catholic Majesty see how to remedy the error committed thus far so that Your Catholic Majesty's will may be done regarding our duties and those of the collectors. From the *indios* we get nothing; we only have what we make in our houses and fields, to which they contribute nothing. Nor do they have anything to contribute, because they lack the sense to live, as indeed they do. Let Your Holy Majesty decide how you can best be served.

Now, wanting to be ordained as I do, if I join the clergy they want to take away the *indios* that were given to me. Let your Sacred Majesty judge how unfair it is that the sixty *indios* (more or less) that I finally received after twenty years have been taken from me, just one day after taking possession of them and before they were able to serve me. They say that Your Holy Majesty does not want the clergy to have *indios*. They were not given to me as a cleric but as a conquistador, as I have reminded Your Catholic Majesty above. I beg Your Majesty that this affront not take place in my lifetime, because it would mean not paying me for some of my labor. Instead, Your Sacred Majesty should grant this favor, as I have already begged Your Majesty above. May Your Sacred Majesty provide that your loyal vassals and servants be compensated somehow. Even if we are not compensated as Your Catholic Majesty should wish, may it at least be according to the time, place, and season that best serve Our Lord and Your Holy Majesty. I request nothing more from Your Catholic Majesty. I can only say that there is nothing in this land that could be sent to whoever would request it. Since my request is fair and reasonable, may Your Catholic Majesty grant me mercy and grace as you grant to the poor. I trust that it will be so and that my bold and fair request will be heard. Thus, I remain praying to God Our Lord to guard and extend the days of Your Holy Catholic Cesarean Majesty, as I and your loyal vassals and servants wish. From Nuestra Señora de Asunción, on the second day of July, in the year 1556.

103. Located in the port city of Seville, the Casa de la Contratación, or House of Trade, administered all overseas voyages and trade, as well as the collection of the royal fifth due to the crown. On the Casa de la Contratación see Parry (1990, 54–58).

This I say, because it is the truth, as those who go there will attest, unless they die. My writing is only as rhetorical and elegant as Your Holy Majesty sees and hears.

Your Catholic Cesarean Majesty's humble
and loyal vassal and servant,
Domingo Martínez

Epilogue

The establishment of an *encomienda* system in 1556 marked the beginning of the colonial period in the Río de la Plata. Once the dream of discovering the Sierra de la Plata was abandoned, the Spaniards of Asunción set out to make the best of what they had. The would-be conquistadors sought to become capitalists by exploiting the labor of the Guaraní, who would no longer be regarded as allies but as serfs—a role that the Guaraní resisted for decades. However, the region remained an impoverished backwater. Besides being sparsely populated by unruly natives, the region had no gold or silver mines, and the soil could not support extensive sugarcane plantations. The settlers lived on what they managed to grow, and the economy was based on barter rather than cash—though fishhooks, iron wedges, and knives were used as a sort of currency. As there were no profitable resources, no surplus, and no money, there were also no new settlers. Moreover, direct communication with Spain was mostly severed because official matters were increasingly handled through the Viceroyalty of Peru.[1] The contentious political environment, however, remained unchanged.

Domingo de Irala had been the leader of Asunción for almost twenty years. Even when he was not acting governor, his actions greatly influenced the life of the colony. His passing left an unfillable void. Irala's appointed successor was his son-in-law, Gonzalo de Mendoza, who died unexpectedly two years later. In 1558, the city's *cabildo* decided to call for an election, which was possible by virtue of the 1537 royal decree.[2] Another of Irala's sons-in-law, Francisco

---

1. The Viceroyalty of Peru was officially established in 1542; it gained jurisdictional authority over all the provinces to the south until the creation of the Viceroyalty of the Río de la Plata in 1777.

2. This was the decree brought to the Río de la Plata by Alonso Cabrera in 1539 that allowed the conquistadors to elect their own leader if the formal chain of

Ortiz de Vergara, was elected as lieutenant governor, pending royal confirmation. Guaraní revolts coincided with this change of power and with the next major setback for the colony: in 1564, approximately three hundred Spanish settlers and an unspecified number of *mestizos* left Asunción to follow Nuflo de Chávez to Santa Cruz de la Sierra. Chávez had founded a town three years earlier halfway between Ciudad de los Reyes (Lima) in Peru and Asunción to serve as the capital of the newly created province of Chiquitos, as an extension of the Viceroyalty of Peru. Governor Ortiz de Vergara joined the expedition with the goal of meeting with the Viceroy.

Once the expedition reached Santa Cruz, Ortiz de Vergara was arrested and charged with abandoning his governorship without royal authorization.[3] In his stead, the authorities in Lima designated the rich *encomendero* Juan Ortiz de Zárate, who among other things had promised to deliver four thousand heads of cattle, four thousand sheep, five hundred horses, five hundred goats, and three hundred men to the Río de la Plata. Ortiz de Zárate immediately set out for Spain to obtain confirmation from King Philip II, charging the quarrelsome *contador* Felipe de Cáceres to go back to Asunción as his lieutenant governor. In 1568, Cáceres took charge of the province, which quickly fell into chaos once again because of the continual power struggle between Lieutenant Governor Cáceres and Bishop Fernández de la Torre. The turmoil lasted until the bishop managed to have Cáceres seized and shipped back to Spain in 1572.[4] Three years later, having secured the titles of *adelantado*, governor, and captain general of the Río de la Plata, Ortiz de Zárate finally managed to make his way back to Asunción only to die soon after, leaving his promises to supply cattle and men mostly unfulfilled.[5]

Ortiz de Zárate had bequeathed his governorship and titles to whoever married his daughter Juana, who had remained in Peru. Until then, his nephew Diego Ortiz de Zárate y Mendieta was to

---

command had been broken. The decree was not put into effect at the time because Cabrera recognized Irala as Juan de Ayolas's designated successor.

3. The likely authors of this plot were Chávez and Felipe de Cáceres, the *contador* who many years before had conspired against Álvar Núñez Cabeza de Vaca.

4. Fernández de la Torre went along but died en route; Cáceres reached Spain, where he was tried and acquitted of any wrongdoing. The interim governor from 1572 and 1575 was one Martín Suárez de Toledo.

5. Aboard Ortiz de Zárate's fleet were Fray Alonso de San Buenaventura and Fray Luis de Bolaños, the founders of the first religious missions in the Río de la Plata.

serve as interim governor. However, Mendieta's arrogance led to his deposition within a few months of his appointment. Meanwhile, the *adelantado's* lieutenant general, Juan de Garay, was in Peru hastening the marriage between Juana Ortiz de Zárate and Juan Torres de Vera y Aragón, who in 1577 became the sixth person to hold the title of *adelantado* of the Río de la Plata.[6] Garay returned to Asunción in 1578 to take over as lieutenant governor, a post he held until his untimely death in 1583. At that time, Torres de Vera was still tied up in litigation over his right to the governorship in Peru, so he sent his cousin Juan Torres de Navarrete to replace Garay. Governor Torres de Vera did not arrive in Asunción until 1587—three years after his wife's passing. The *adelantado* and his lieutenants, most of whom were his relatives, soon fell out with the colonists, who accused them of abusing their power. After he defied several warnings, the crown rescinded Torres de Vera's titles in 1593. Torres de Vera was the last *adelantado* of the Río de la Plata.

Paraguayan historian Luis Benítez (1985, 77) highlights the fact that it was not the *adelantados*, but their lieutenants who were responsible for the advancement of the colony over the course of the sixteenth century. Nonetheless, as Benítez (1985, 78) also notes, after decades of struggle, by the end of the "age of *adelantados*" the Spanish presence in the region was securely established. After Juan de Garay refounded the port of Buenos Aires in 1580, Asunción began to lose its former importance as the central hub of the colonial enterprise in the Río de la Plata. In effect, Buenos Aires was already the capital city in 1607, when Governor Hernandarias de Saavedra insisted on the convenience of splitting the province.[7] In 1617, King Philip III demarcated the governorship of Paraguay, with Asunción as its capital, from the governorship of the Río de la Plata, with Buenos Aires as its capital. Paradoxically, the division signals the ultimate success of an endeavor that started with the odds heavily stacked against it.

The letters included in this volume call attention to a highly original chapter in the history of Latin America that has been unduly

6. Pedro de Mendoza, Álvar Núñez Cabeza de Vaca, Juan de Sanabria, Diego de Sanabria, and Juan Ortiz de Zárate were his predecessors. Neither Juan de Sanabria nor his son Diego ever made it to the Río de la Plata.

7. Generally called Hernandarias, Hernando Arias de Saavedra (1561–1634) has the distinction of being the first American-born governor of the province.

neglected. They were written at the most crucial junctures of the conquest of the Río de la Plata. The constant state of crisis they reveal contests the triumphalist view of the Spanish conquest found in more formal histories. Written by assorted individuals, they highlight the diversity of the conquistadors. Along with the men bearing swords or crosses, there were women like Isabel de Guevara and craftsmen such as Domingo Martínez whose contributions were equally important. Their letters also show that all were human in their fears, hopes, and motivations. And although there are no indigenous voices as such, it is possible to tease out the complex relationship between settlers and natives. The fact that the Spaniards managed to colonize the Río de la Plata despite countless mishaps indicates not only great determination, but great adaptability as well. On the other hand, the fact that all along, despite heavy pressure, the Guaraní were able to influence the terms of engagement demonstrates comparable fortitude and flexibility. Both groups' peculiar modes of interaction determined the course of this particular conquest. Many of its features correspond to a general pattern, but its idiosyncrasies underscore that it is misleading to speak of the *Conquista* of America. There were in fact many conquests whose outcomes were determined by myriad local factors, including among others distance, weather, politics, and local culture. Considering the conditions in which it began, the conquest of the Río de la Plata was an especially improbable feat.

adelantado   Military commander of a discovery, conquest, and colonizing expedition. *Adelantados* had the right to distribute gains and to
appoint officers. Once a settlement was founded, the *adelantado* generally acted as governor; his officers often became political appointees.

alcalde mayor   Chief magistrate of a municipality for both criminal and
civil matters. *Alcaldes* were generally elected by the *cabildo*, but *adelantados* could appoint the *alcalde* of a new settlement. The authority
of the office was signified by a ceremonial rod.

alguacil   Constable in charge of administering justice. The *alguacil mayor*
was the chief constable and bore the royal staff of justice.

cabildo   Municipal council. The *cabildo* had judicial, legislative, and admin-
istrative functions. Depending on the size of the municipality, *cabildo*
officials included several *regidores*, who represented the heads of
household, one or two *alcaldes*, the *alguacil mayor*, and a *procurador*.

cacique   Indigenous leader. Derived from the Arawak word for "ruler," the
term *cacique* became widely used in Spanish America.

canónigo   Canon. The *canónigo* is a member of a cathedral's chapter
(assembly) trained in canon law and tasked with counseling the bishop.

capitulación (pl. *capitulaciones*)   A contract between the crown and an
individual wishing to undertake a discovery and settlement or trading
venture, generally at his own expense. In exchange for a fifth of all
gross revenue, the crown granted titles and privileges commensurate
with the profits expected form the enterprise.

comisario (religious)   In the New World, the head of a Franciscan mission.

conquista   Conquest. In the New World, a *conquista* had both a military
and a religious component because evangelization served as its osten-
sive justification. Thus, a conquering expedition usually included one
or more representatives of the clergy. The rest of the crew consisted
of an assortment of individuals from all walks of life seeking to make
their fortune across the sea.

contador   Accountant. The *contador* was one of the royal officials, along
with the *tesorero*, the *factor*, and the *veedor*. The *contador* was in
charge of bookkeeping.

encomienda   A grant of a number of *indios* to an individual Spaniard, called
an *encomendero*, who was supposed to ensure their protection and

religious instruction. In return, the *encomendero* was entitled to collect tribute from his charges, or *indios encomendados*. In practice, the *encomienda* subjected the natives to serfdom.

entrada   Entry. An armed inland expedition for the purpose of exploration and, whenever possible, plunder.

factor   Commercial agent. One of the royal officials, the *factor* was in charge of all in-kind income, including the storing and selling of merchandise. The *factor* was also responsible for the weapon and ammunition stores.

fiscal   Government attorney. The *fiscal* represented the crown's interests in civil disputes and served as prosecutor in criminal cases.

hacienda   Productive land. The term *hacienda* comprises the notions of land, labor, and wealth, including livestock.

indio   Native American. The blanket term *indio* had derogatory connotations, whether it be savagery or docility, guile or gullibility. An indigenous leader was an *indio principal*, often abbreviated to *principal*.

licenciado   Licentiate. A *licenciado* was someone with a master's degree, generally in law, whether civil or canon law.

maestre de campo   Second in command of an expedition. The *maestre de campo* was in charge of logistics and maintaining order through the administration of justice.

mestizo   The offspring of a Spaniard and an *india*. The term *mestizo* was almost synonymous with illegitimacy, which entailed a variety of social obstacles and restrictions. Nevertheless, Spaniards would sometimes look after the welfare of their *mestizo* children and even recognize them.

procurador   Attorney. A person empowered to speak on behalf of an individual or a group and act in their name was called a *procurador*. The *procurador* could serve as both advocate and defense attorney.

provisión (pl. *provisiones*)   A judicial order that commanded the implementation of a royal decree. Sometimes, colonial officials would refuse to comply with a *provisión* if its enactment was perceived to be counterproductive or overly contentious.

provisor   Cathedral chapter's judge. The *provisor* was appointed by a bishop to serve in his name as judge in an ecclesiastical court.

tesorero   Treasurer. One of the royal officials, the *tesorero* oversaw the treasury and was responsible for collecting and making payments.

regidor   Alderman. The *regidores* were municipal representatives who served in the *cabildo*; their number depended on the size of the municipality.

repartimiento   Distribution. The *repartimiento* could refer to the distribution of plunder among conquistadors, of land among settlers, and of *indios* (as in an *encomienda*) or conscripted *indio* labor among colonists.

requerimiento   Requirement. A *requerimiento* is a judicial demand to execute a task or, contrarily, to refrain from it. It may also be an official demand for a position statement or an answer to a given question. The most famous *requerimiento* was formulated by Spanish jurist Juan López de Palacios Rubios in 1513. The text, which conquistadors were to read aloud before engaging an indigenous population, demanded unconditional submission to God and the king of Castile, threatening war without mercy in case of noncompliance.

veedor   Inspector. One the royal officials, the *veedor* had the task of looking after the crown's interests by collecting its share of income and by overseeing the smelting of gold and silver.

Adorno, Rolena, and Patrick C. Pautz. 1999. *Álvar Núñez Cabeza de Vaca: His Account, His Life, and the Expedition of Pánfilo de Narváez.* Lincoln: University of Nebraska Press.

Arnaud, Vicente Guillermo. 1950. *Los intérpretes en el descubrimiento, conquista y colonización del Río de la Plata.* Buenos Aires: Talleres Gráficos Didot.

Becco, Horacio Jorge, ed. 1994. *Cronistas del Río de la Plata.* Caracas: Biblioteca Ayacucho.

Benítez, Luis G. 1985. *Historia del Paraguay: Época colonial.* Asunción: Imprenta Comuneros.

Bolaños, Álvaro Félix. 2002. "The Requirements of a Memoir: Ulrich Schmidel's Account of the Conquest of the River Plate (1536–54)." *Colonial Latin American Review* 11, no. 2: 231–50.

Brading, D. A. 1993. *First America: Spanish Monarchy, Creole Patriots and the Liberal State, 1492–1866.* Cambridge: Cambridge University Press.

Burns, E. Bradford. 1993. *A History of Brazil.* New York: Columbia University Press.

Bustos Rodríguez, Manuel. 1985. "Oligarquía urbana y negocio mercantil en el Cádiz de la edad moderna: El clan de los Villavicencio." *Anales de la Universidad de Cádiz* 2: 175–89.

Cardozo, Efraím. 1959. *El Paraguay colonial: Las raíces de la nacionalidad.* Buenos Aires: Nizza.

———. 1989. *El Paraguay de la conquista.* Asunción: El Lector.

Cartas De Indias. 1877. Madrid: Impr. de Manuel G. Hernández.

Chinchilla, Rosa Helena. 2004. "Juana of Austria: Courtly Spain and Devotional Expression." *Renaissance and Reformation* 28, no. 1: 21–33.

Díaz de Guzmán, Ruy. 1986. *La Argentina.* Edited by Enrique de Gandía. Madrid: Historia 16.

Documentos históricos y geográficos relativos a la conquista y colonización rioplatense. 1941. Comisión nacional del IV centenario de la primera fundación de Buenos Aires, 1536–1936. 5 vols. Buenos Aires: Talleres S. A. Casa Jacobo Peuser.

Dominguez, Luis L., ed. 2010 (1891). *The Conquest of the River Plate (1535–1555).* Cambridge: Cambridge University Press.

Elliott, John H. 2002. *Imperial Spain, 1469–1716.* London: Penguin.

Gandía, Enrique de. 1932a. *Historia de la conquista del Río de la Plata y del Paraguay: Los gobiernos de don Pedro de Mendoza, Álvar Núñez y Domingo de Irala, 1535–1556*. Buenos Aires: Librería de A. García Santos.

———. 1932b. *Indios y conquistadores en el Paraguay*. Buenos Aires: Librería de A. García Santos.

———. 1935. *Antecedentes diplomáticos de las expediciones de Juan Díaz de Solís, Sebastián Caboto y don Pedro de Mendoza*. Buenos Aires: Cabaut y Cía.

———. 1936a. *Crónica del magnífico adelantado don Pedro de Mendoza*. Buenos Aires: L. J. Rosso.

———. 1936b. *Historia de Alonso Cabrera y de la destrucción de Buenos Aires en 1541*. Buenos Aires: Librería Cervantes.

Ganson, Barbara Anne. 2005. *The Guaraní Under Spanish Rule in the Río de la Plata*. Stanford: Stanford University Press.

Hanke, Lewis. 1949. *The Spanish Struggle for Justice in the Conquest of America*. Philadelphia: University of Pennsylvania Press.

Kamen, Henry. 2003. *Empire: How Spain Became a World Power, 1492–1763*. New York: HarperCollins.

Keen, Benjamin. 1969. "The Black Legend Revisited: Assumptions and Realities." *Hispanic American Historical Review* 49, no. 4: 703–19.

Konetzke, Richard. 1945. "La emigración de mujeres españolas a América." *Revista Internacional de Sociología* 3, nos. 9–10: 123–50.

———. 1952. *La emigración española al Río de la Plata durante el siglo XVI*. Madrid: Consejo Superior de Investigaciones Científicas.

Lafuente Machaín, Ricardo de. 1939. *El gobernador Domingo Martínez de Irala*. Buenos Aires: Bernabé y Cía.

———. 1943. *Los conquistadores del Río de la Plata*. 2nd ed. Buenos Aires: Ayacucho.

Laguarda Trías, Rolando A. 1988. "Pilotos portugueses en el Rio de la Plata durante el siglo XVI." *Revista da universidade de Coimbra* 34: 57–84.

Lockhart, James, and Enrique Otte, eds. 1976. *Letters and People of the Spanish Indies: Sixteenth Century*. Cambridge: Cambridge University Press.

López de Gómara, Francisco. 1979. *Historia general de las Indias y Vida de Hernán Cortés*. Edited by Jorge Gurría Lacroix. Caracas: Ayacucho.

Lopreto, Gladys. 1996. ". . . que vivo en ésta conquista." *Textos del Río de la Plata, siglo XVI*. Buenos Aires: Universidad Nacional de La Plata.

Lynch, John. 1964. *Spain Under the Habsburgs*. New York: Oxford University Press.

Maura, Juan Francisco. 2005. *Españolas de ultramar en la historia y en la literatura*. Valencia: Universitat de València.

———. 2008. *El gran burlador de América: Álvar Núñez Cabeza de Vaca*. Madrid: Parnaseo.

McCreery, David. 2000. *The Sweat of Their Brow: A History of Work in Latin America*. Armonk, N.Y.: M. E. Sharpe.

Medina, José Toribio. 1908. *El portugués Gonzalo de Acosta al servicio de España: Estudio histórico*. Santiago de Chile: Imprenta Elzeviriana.

Necker, Louis. 1974. "La réaction des Indiens Guarani à la Conquête espagnole du Paraguay, un des facteurs de la colonisation de l'Argentine à la fin du XVIe siècle." *Bulletin de la Société Suisse des Américanistes* 38: 71–80.

———. 1979. *Indiens Guarani et chamanes franciscains: Les premières réductions du Paraguay, 1580–1800*. Paris: Anthropos.

Nowell, Charles E. 1946. "Aleixo García and the White King." *Hispanic American Historical Review* 26, no. 4: 450–66.

Núñez Cabeza de Vaca, Álvar, and Pedro Hernández. 1906. *Relación de los naufragios y comentarios de Álvar Núñez Cabeza De Vaca*. Edited by Manuel Serrano y Sanz. 2 vols. Madrid: Victoriano Suárez.

Núñez Cabeza de Vaca, Álvar. 2011. *The South American Expeditions, 1540–1545*. Translated by Baker H. Murrow. Albuquerque: University of New Mexico Press.

Parry, John H. 1990. *The Spanish Seaborne Empire*. Berkeley: University of California Press.

Rípodas Ardanaz, Daisy. 1987. "Movimientos shamánicos de liberación entre los Guaraníes (1545–1660)." *Teología* 50: 245–75.

Rivarola Paoli, Juan Bautista. 1986. *La economía colonial*. Asunción: Litocolor.

Rodríguez Molas, Ricardo. 1985. *Los sometidos de la conquista: Argentina, Bolivia, Paraguay*. Buenos Aires: Centro Editor de América Latina.

Roulet, Florencia. 1993. *La resistencia de los guaraní del Paraguay a la conquista española (1537–1556)*. Misiones, Argentina: Universidad Nacional de Misiones.

Schmidel, Ulrico. 1986. *Relatos de la conquista del Río de la Plata y Paraguay, 1534–1554*. Translated by Klaus Wagner. Madrid: Alianza.

Schmidl, Ulrico. 1948. *Crónica del viaje a las regiones del Plata, Paraguay y Brasil*. Translated by Edmundo Wernicke. Buenos Aires: Talleres Peuser.

Schwaller, John F. 2011. *The History of the Catholic Church in Latin America: From Conquest to Revolution and Beyond*. New York: New York University Press.

Scott, Nina M. 1999. *Madres del verbo = Mothers of the Word: Early Spanish-American Women Writers: A Bilingual Anthology*. Albuquerque: University of New Mexico Press.

Service, Elman R. 1951. "The Encomienda in Paraguay." *Hispanic American Historical Review* 31, no. 2: 230–52.

———. 1971. *Spanish–Guarani Relations in Early Colonial Paraguay*. Westport, Conn.: Greenwood Press.

Susnik, Branislava. 1965–66. *El indio colonial del Paraguay*. 2 vols. Asunción: Museo etnográfico Andrés Barbero.

Tuer, Dorothy Jane. 2011. "Tigers and Crosses: The Transcultural Dynamics of Spanish–Guaraní Relations in the Río de la Plata: 1516–1580." Ph.D. diss., University of Toronto.

Vargas Ugarte, Rubén. 1951–54. *Concilios limenses (1551–1772)*. 3 vols. Lima: Tipografía Peruana.

Verdesio, Gustavo. 2001. *Forgotten Conquests: Rereading New World History from the Margins*. Philadelphia: Temple University Press.

Zavala, Silvio. 1977. *Orígenes de la colonización en el Río de la Plata*. Mexico City: Colegio Nacional.

Page numbers in *italics* indicate figures.

Abreu [Abrego], Diego d', 12, 63–64, 88, 89, 90
Acosta, Gonzalo de, 18–19, 51, 67
Acosta, Gregorio de, 67n63
Acuña, Hector de, 20
adelantados
  crown efforts to control, xiin1
  last, 103
  list of, 103n6
  negotiation of *capitulaciones* (contracts) by, 29
Agreda, Martín de. *See* Pavón, Juan, letter to Martín de Agreda
Alexander VI (pope), 2–3, 68
Almagro, Diego de, 32, 32n8, 33, 33n11
Alvarado, Pedro de, 33, 33n11
Alvares Cabral, Pedro, 18, 18n29
Andrada, Francisco de
  arrival in Río de la Plata, 69
  on Asunción, native culture in, 70
  career of, 69
  on enslavement of natives, 74
  faith-based interpretative frame of, 66
  and Irala, 66–67, 71–72
  letter to Council of the Indies, 69–76; notable features of, 25, 65–69
  on natives: eagerness for conversion, 66, 67, 70, 72–73; effort to educate and convert, 67, 71–73; immoral practices of, 66, 70, 71, 73; and marriage, monogamous, as issue, 67–68, 68n65, 73; on shamans' opposition to Christianity, 67, 72
  and politics of colony, 66–67
  request for bishop status and income, 68, 75–76
request for punishment of bad priests, 75
request for royal support, 73–74, 75
requests for church supplies, 68, 74–75
on Spaniards: immoral behavior of, 66, 67, 74: relations with native women as practical necessity, 66, 74
Angulo, Antonio de, 32
Apiraes people, 80
Aracare (*indio principal*), 52
La Argentina (Díaz de Guzmán), 2
Argentine historiography, focus of, 1
Arrieta, Ana de, 35
Asunción, *xiii*
  Andrada on, 70
  Cabeza de Vaca's arrival in, 10, 59
  as capital of governorship of Paraguay, 103
  Chaves party departure from, 102
  de la Torre's arrival in, 91, 91n98
  early hardship in, 42, 56, 70–71
  establishment of, 7, 7n14, 22, 31n5
  fire (February, 1543), 52
  locust plague at, 46, 66, 70
  move upriver to, xii, 9, 42
  native culture in, 70
  refounding of Buenos Aires (1580) and, 103
Atahualpa, 4, 4n9
Ayolas, Juan de
  death, reports of, 7–8, 48, 51, 58
  disappearance of, xii, 7–8, 43, 45–46, 56; Irala's assumption of leadership following, xii, 57; struggle for power following, 8, 9, 43, 47, 51
  entradas by, 6, 7–8, 45, 56, 57–58
  as governor, appointment of, 7, 47
  Mendoza letter to, 30–34; notable features of, 23, 29–30; as undelivered, 30

Andrada, Francisco de (cont'd)
    search for, 8–9, 21, 43, 44, 46–48, 49,
        50, 57–58, 87

Balboa, Vasco Núñez de, 3n5
Benítez, Luis, 103
Bolañus, Luis de, 102n5
Brazil, discovery of, 3n6, 18, 18n29
Buena Esperanza fort, 6
Buenos Aires, xiii
    abandonment of, xii, 9, 31n4, 49–50;
        Galán on, 58–59; Irala and, 9, 24,
        31n4, 43, 49–50, 58–59
    Domingo Martínez in, 93
    food shortages in, 48, 49
    founding of, 6–7
    Galán as lieutenant governor in, 7,
        31n6, 43, 46
    Mendoza in, 5n10, 6–7, 56
    port facilities, 48, 48–49n30
    refounding of (1580), 17, 103
    siege of, 6, 23

Cabeza de Vaca, Álvar Núñez
    arrival in Río de la Plata, 9–10, 15, 49,
        50–51, 59
    assumption of governor's office, xii, 51
    colonists arriving with, 37, 42n21
    Comentarios by, 2, 22n37
    entradas by, 10–11, 52–53, 59
    in Florida, 9–10
    and Guaraní, relations with, 15–16
    interpreter and guide of, 19
    Irala's claimed support for, 44, 50–53
    killing of Aracare, 52
    plots against, Galán on, 59
    relación of, 10n17
    relatives of, 54
    removal and arrest of, 10–11, 24, 53,
        62; abuses by Irala following, 76, 77,
        78, 80–91; accusations against, 11,
        11n19, 53; Andrada on, 67; Galán
        on, 55, 59–60; Irala's assumption
        of power following, xii, 53; Irala's
        explanation of, 24, 44, 53; Irala's
        necessity of defending, 24, 43; legal
        proceedings against perpetrators
        of, 54; Martín González on, 78–80;
        Pavón on, 62–63
    sources on administration of, 2

    trial of, Galán on, 55, 60
Cabot, Sebastian, 4, 18, 20
Cabrera, Alonso
    and abandonment of Buenos Aires
        settlement, 9, 49–50
    arrival in Río de la Plata, 8, 49, 69n69
    as captain of the Santiago, 5n10
    and command of colony, 47
    and decree allowing elections, 101–2n2
    and deposing of Cabeza de Vaca, 62
    Galán on, 57
Cáceres, Felipe de
    as contador, 32, 32n7
    and deposing of Ortiz de Vergara,
        102n3
    as lieutenant governor, 63, 89, 90, 102;
        and Cabeza de Vaca, arrest of, 53, 62;
        executions under, 37n16
    and Mendoza entrata from Peru,
        84–85
    power struggle with de la Torre, 102
    return to Spain, 19n30
Cáceres, Juan de, 32, 32n7
La Candelaria (port), xiii, 7–8, 45, 46, 47,
        48, 56, 57
cannibalism
    by hungry colonists, 6, 35
    by natives, Andrada on, 70, 71, 72
capitulaciones (contracts), governors'
        negotiation of, 29
Cardoza, Efraím, 1n3
Cario people
    as allies of settlers, 13, 15, 46, 57, 85, 86
    neighboring peoples, 14
    uprising of, 80–81
Casa de Contratación, 98, 98n103
Chané people, 14, 48, 57, 58, 85
Charles V (king of Spain), 18–19, 37,
        61, 69. See also González, Martín,
        letter to Charles V; Irala, Domingo
        Martínez de, letter to Charles V;
        Martínez, Domingo, letter to
        Charles V
Charrúa people, 14
Chaves, Nuflo [Nufrio] de, 11, 85, 85n94,
        87, 90–91, 102, 102n3
Chinchilla, Rosa Helena, 37
Chiquitos province, 102
Christianity, Guaraní backlash against,
        16–17, 67, 72

Cimeonos people, 87
Ciudad Real, establishment of, 17
Columbus, Christopher, 34
Comentarios (Cabeza de Vaca), 2, 22n37
comuneros revolt (1520-21), 61
conquest of Americas, multiple conquests within, 104
conquistadors
    adherence to judicial procedures, 30
    conflict with religious goals of colonies, 25
    diversity of, 104
    immoral behavior of, Andrada on, 25, 66, 67, 74
    resourcefulness and resoluteness of, 45, 104
contracts (capitulaciones), governors' negotiation of, 29
Corocotoques people, 87
Coronucocies people, 59
Corpus Christi, 6, 7, 22, 41n19, 56
Council of the Indies, Andrada letter to, 69–76
    notable features of, 25, 65–69
craftsmen in Río de la Plata, 93–95, 104
Cromberger, Jacobo, 75n83

Dávila, María, 35
de la Torre, Pedro Fernández, 13, 19, 91, 91n98, 102
de Vera de Villavicencio, Rodrigo. See Galán, Francisco, letter to Rodrigo de Vera
Díaz de Guzmán, Ruy, 2
Díaz de Solís, Juan, 3, 3n5, 20
Domingo (indio principal), 49

electoral experiment of Río de la Plata, 8, 101, 101–2n2
encomiendas
    as anachronistic, 36
    bending of law on, 36, 36n14, native resistance to
    clerics' ownership of, as prohibited, 92, 98
    colonists' dissatisfaction with, 35, 42
    creation of, as beginning of colonial period, 101
    Domingo Martínez's effort to retain, 92, 95, 98

duration of, as issue, 36, 36n15
    as fallback plan of colonists, 13n22, 101
    granting of, 16, 95
    Guaraní resistance to, 16–17, 101
    impact on Guaraní people, 16
    Irala's promises of, 12, 13, 89
    Isabel de Guevara on, 35
    as only source of wealth in colony, 35
    regulations governing, 36nn14–15
    small size of, 13n22, 35
    unequal distribution of, 35, 64, 91
Entigura, 67, 72
Escaso, Antón Martín, 63–64
Esquivel, Pedro de, 36–37, 37n16, 42, 42n21
Estopiñán, Catalina de, 54, 61

feitorias, importance to Spanish mission, 18
Felipe II (king of Spain), 19
First Council of Lima (1551-52), 68n65
Franciscan missionaries, 17–18, 68. See also missionaries
Fustes, Juan de, 20

Galán, Francisco
    allegiance to Cabeza de Vaca, 54
    on Alonso Cabrera, 57
    on Ayolas, 8, 56–57, 57–58
    on Buenos Aires abandonment, 58–59
    on Cabeza de Vaca, 55, 59–60
    criticisms of Mendoza and captains, 54–55, 55–56
    on hardships of colonists, 55, 56, 58
    on Irala, 24, 57–58, 58–59
    letter to Rodrigo de Vera, 55–61; notable features of, 24, 54–55
    as well-connected, 54
Gandía, Enrique de, 2, 5, 5n10
Garay, Juan de, 103
García, Alejo, 20n34, 45, 52
    former slave of, 45, 48, 51, 56
García de Moguer, Diego, 4, 18
Gasca, Pedro de la, 64n55
Gijuy (port), 52
Gomez, Jorge, 18
González, Bartolomé, 63
González, Martín
    distancing of self from conquistadors, 76

González, Martín (cont'd)
  hyperbole of, 76
  on Irala: Abreu [Abrego] revolt against,
    88, 89, 90; as anticrown rebel, 79;
    mistreatment of natives by, 25, 76,
    77, 78, 80–87, 88–89, 90–91; and
    native women, sexual exploitation
    of, 76, 77, 80, 81, 82, 88, 89, 90, 91;
    as source of revolt against Cabeza
    de Vaca, 78–80; suppression of critics
    by, 88–89; torture of ineffective
    native guides by, 85, 86
  letter to Charles V, 78–91; notable
    features of, 76–78
  and native culture, imperfect percep-
    tion of, 77–78
  on native shamans, 16
  on native women, humanity of, 77
government of Río de la Plata. See also
    adelantados; judicial procedures
    after death of Irala, 101–3
  chain of command, frequent disruption
    of, 44
  infighting in, ubiquity of, xi
  political struggle after disappearance
    of Ayolas, 8, 9, 43, 47, 51; Irala's
    deemphasis of, 43, 46n28
grants and titles from king, as tradable
    goods, 29
Guaraní culture, 14–15
  burial customs, 78
  influence on Paraguan culture, 22–23,
    78, 104
  labor obligations in, 36
  and missionaries' accommodation
    strategy, 67–68
  traditional marriage, 14, 15; and family
    ties to colonists, 15, 77–78; Spanish
    failure to honor, 15–16
Guaraní people, 13–18. See also natives
  area inhabited by, 14
  backlash against Christianity, 16–17,
    67, 72
  conquest of, factors allowing for, 15, 17
  and encomiendas, 16–17, 101
  and Irala, support of, 52
  and killing of Aracare, 52
  lack of centralized power, 17
  missionaries' views of, as eager for
    conversion, 66

neighboring peoples, 14
  origin of, 13
  and reducciones, 17–18
  relations with colonists: collapse of,
    15–17; early support, 7, 13, 15, 46
  resourcefulness and resoluteness of,
    104
  social and linguistic homogeneity of, 15
  Spanish attacks on, 52
  uprisings by, 16–17, 52, 102
Guatatas people, 80
Guaycurú people, 16
Guevara, Isabel de
  arrival in Río de la Plata, 41
  compensation for husband requested
    by, 36–37, 42
  and diversity of conquistadors, 104
  on encomiendas distribution, 35, 42
  on hardships of colonists, 23–24, 35,
    41–42
  increased compensation requested by,
    36, 42
  letter to Princess Juana, 41–43; manu-
    script of, 38–40; notable features of,
    23, 34–37
  and male honor, concern for, 35
  as only women to write letter in Río de
    la Plata colony, 35
  on women's contributions to early
    colony, 23–24, 35, 41–42
guides and interpreters
  control of information flow by, 22
  cultural knowledge of, 22
  importance to Spanish mission, 18–23
  ineffective, Irala's torture of, 85, 86
  linguistic homogeneity of Guaraní and,
    15
  ongoing legacy of, 22–23
  religious education of natives and, 67
Gutierres, Elvira, 35
Gutierres, Leonor, 35
Guzmán, Alonso Ríquel de, 12

hardships of colonists, 6
  Andrada on, 66
  Galán on, 55, 56, 58
  hunger, 6, 23, 35, 41, 55, 56
  illness, 6–7, 23–24, 48, 49, 53, 58, 59,
    71, 79
  Irala on, 44, 48, 49, 53

Isabel de Guevara on, 23–24, 35, 41–42
Martín González on, 79
Pedro de Mendoza on, 23
Hernández, Pedro, 59
Hernández, Pero, 2
historiographic sources on Río de la Plata,
1–2

incest by natives, Andrada on, 70, 71, 73
Inter caetera (1493 papal bull), 2–3
interpreters. *See* guides and interpreters
Irala, Domingo Martínez de
Abreu [Abrego] revolt against, 12,
63–64, 88, 89
abuses, complaints about, xii, 13, 24;
Galán on, 58–59; González on, 76,
77, 78, 80–87, 88–91; Irala's suppres-
sion of, 13, 63, 88–89, 90; Pavón on,
52, 61–65
appointment as governor, xii, 8, 12–13,
64, 91
and Ayolas, disappearance of, 45–46,
56; assumption of leadership following, xii, 57; reported death of, 7–8,
48, 51, 58; search for, 8–9, 43, 44,
46–48, 49, 50, 57–58, 87; struggle for
power following, 8, 9, 43, 47, 51
as Ayolas' *maestre de campo*, 7
and Buenos Aires abandonment, 9,
24, 31n4, 43, 49–50; explanation of,
49–50; Galán on, 58–59
and Cabeza de Vaca: claimed loyalty
and support for, 44, 50–53; *maestre
de campo* of, 10; murder of Aracare
ordered by, 52
and Cabeza de Vaca's removal, 11, 62;
Abreu [Abrego] counterrevolt, 12,
63–64, 88, 89; assumption of power
following, xii, 53; explanation of, 24,
44, 53; Martín González on, 78–80;
necessity of defending, 24, 43
death of, 13, 101
and *encomiendas*: colonists' dissat-
isfaction with, 35; granting of, 16,
95; promises of, 12, 13, 89; unequal
distribution of, 35, 64, 91
entradas by, 7, 11–12, 16, 37, 51–52,
57, 59, 63, 64, 89–90, 91; destruction caused by, 81–87, 89–90; loss of
command during, 12, 87

exaggeration of colonists' success by, 9,
50
favoring of supporters by, 35, 63, 64,
79, 80, 82, 86, 88, 91
food shortages and, 48, 49
Galán on, 57–58, 58–59
greed of, González on, 82
Guaraní perception of, 16
on hardships of colonists, 44, 48, 49, 53
harshness of punishments by, 89–90
and language, openly deceptive use of,
44, 50
letter to Charles V, 45–54; notable
features of, 24, 43–45
native captives taken by, González on,
82–87
on natives, relations with, 44, 46–47,
52
and Peru, delegation sent to, 85n94, 87
and priest, request for, 53–54
property of enemies, seizure and redistribution of, 63
and religious conversion of natives,
support for, 71–72
and Ruiz Galán, struggle for power
with, 8, 9, 47; Irala's de-emphasis of,
43, 46n28
service to crown as claimed motivation
of, 43, 44, 51, 53
sexual abuse of native women,
González on, 76, 77, 80, 81, 82, 88,
89, 90, 91
ship and equipment problems, 46, 50;
torture of ineffective native guides,
85, 86
subduing of native uprising, 52
successor of, 101–2
supplies, requests for, 53

Jesuit missionaries, 1n1, 18, 37, 68, 69n67
Juana de Austria, 37. *See also* Guevara,
Isabel de, letter to Princess Juana
judicial procedures
conquistadors' adherence to, 30, 45
corruption of, 55
as discreetly dispensable, 30, 32
Galán on, 55
Pavón's faith in, 62
Julius II (pope), 68
Justiniano, Bartolomé, 64, 90–91

Kamen, Henry, 35
Konetzke, Richard, 34–35

Lafuente Machaín, Ricardo de, 37n16
Laguarda Trías, Rolando A., 19–20n33
las Casas, Bartolomé de, 36n15, 66n61,
    76n85
letters to Spain
    and historical accuracy, 55
    isolation of settlers and, 55, 69–70
    provenance and publication history,
        26–27
    purposes served by, xi, 24, 29
    style of, 27
    translation of, 27
    and uniqueness of Río de la Plata
        conquest, 103–4
Loaisa, García Jofre de, 4n7
locusts, plague of at Asunción, 46, 66, 70
López de Aguiar, Antonio, 69, 69n69
Los Reyes (port), xiii, 52–53, 59

Magellan, Ferdinand, 3–4
marriage, monogamous, as issue for con-
    verted natives, 67–68, 68n65, 73
Martínez, Domingo
    as craftsman, 25, 93–95, 104
    encomienda of, effort to retain, 92, 95,
        98
    irreverent address to king, 93, 96
    letter to Charles V, 93–99; notable
        features of, 25–26, 92–93
    mestizo daughters, effort to protect, 92,
        95, 96
    on mestizos: danger faced by, 92, 95; as
        potential threat, 26
    on natives, 25–26, 92, 95, 96–97, 98
    plan to become priest, 92, 97, 98
    request for compensation from king,
        95, 96, 98
Maura, Juan Francisco, 34
Mayas [Mbaya], 47, 84–85
Mendoza, Antonio de, 32
Mendoza, Francisco de, 12, 63, 84, 84n92
Mendoza, Gonzalo de, 46, 46n27, 49, 52,
    101
Mendoza, Jorge de, 5
Mendoza, Pedro de (native principal), 73
Mendoza, Pedro de (Spaniard)
    arrival in Río de la Plata, 6

Ayolas as deputy of, 47
    and Ayolas's entrada, 45, 56–57
    as businessman, 29
    capitulacione (contract) negotiated by,
        4–5, 29
    on colonies, moving of, 30–31, 50
    on disciplining of potential traitors,
        xi–xii, 29–30, 32
    entradas by, 6, 56
    as governor, installation of, 4
    guides and interpreters of, 18–19, 20, 21
    on hardships of colonists, 23
    illness and death of, 6–7, 6n13
    injuries sustained by, 31
    instructions on government officials
        and servants, 31–32
    journey to New World, 5–6, 8
    letter to Ayolas, 30–34; notable fea-
        tures of, 23, 29–30
    on profits from colony, distribution of,
        31, 32, 33, 34
    on relations with other Spanish colo-
        nies, 32–33
    return to Spain, 7, 23, 29; power
        struggle following, 77
    on sale of colony, terms for, 33
    subordinates: creation of, 55–56; cri-
        tiques of, 54–55
    wealth of, 4
mestizos
    conquistadors' sexual promiscuity and,
        Andrada on, 66, 74
    Domingo Martínez on: danger faced
        by, 92, 95; mestizo daughters, effort
        to protect, 92, 95, 96; as welcome
        addition, 94
    and expansion of colony, 17
    rights of, restrictions on, 92
    Spanish views on, as potential threat,
        26
Miaracano people, 86
Miguel (nephew of indio Domingo), 49
missionaries. See also Andrada, Francisco
    de; González, Martín; Jesuit mis-
    sionaries; Martínez, Domingo
    accommodation strategy of, 68
    accounts by, greater support as goal of,
        66
    complaints about mistreatment of
        indios, 25

mission and responsibilities of, 25,
65–66
on natives, as eager for conversion, 66,
67, 70, 72–73
and *reducciones*, establishment of, 17–18
Moluccas, Spanish race to claim, 3, 4
Montes, Enrique, 20
Moyganos [Mogranoes] people, 86–87

natives. *See also* Cario people; Guaraní
people; *other specific groups*
agency of, González's perceptions and,
77–78
attacks on other native groups, 48,
80–81, 85–86; motives for, 77
attacks on Spanish settlers, 3, 4, 6, 7–8,
20n34, 51; Irala on, 44, 46–47, 48, 52,
58; Martín González on, 80; women
as combatants in, 41
backlash against Christianity, 16–17,
67, 72
and Cabeza de Vaca, overland travel by,
50–51
culture of: in Asunción, 70; González's
imperfect perception of, 77–78
Domingo Martínez on, 25–26, 92, 95,
96–97, 98
Francisco de Andrada on, 66, 67–68,
68n65, 70–73
immoral practices of, 66, 70, 71, 73
and marriage, monogamous, as issue,
67–68, 68n65, 73
Martínez's relationship with, 25–26
missionaries' views of: as eager for
conversion, 66, 67, 70, 72–73; as
gentle, 66n61
mistreatment of, Martín González on,
25, 76, 77, 78, 80–87, 88–89, 90–91
negative perceptions of, 25, 92, 95,
96–97, 98
religious education and conversion
of: Andrada's efforts in, 67, 71–73;
Church requirements for, 67n62,
72n75; conflict with conquistador's
goals, 25; eagerness for, 66, 67, 70,
72–73; as purported goal of colonies,
65
as serfs under *encomienda* system, 101
Spanish attacks on, 52, 53, 63, 76, 77,
78, 80–87, 88–89, 90–91

Spanish duty to protect, as issue, 36n15
Spanish enslavement of, 63, 74, 83–84,
87
support of Río de la Plata colonists, 6,
7, 10, 51, 53, 56, 59, 70, 86
native women
hiding of from conquistadors, 80, 90
Martín González on, 77
sexual misbehavior with: Andrada on,
66, 74; as contrary to colonial law,
76; Irala and, 76, 77, 80, 81, 82, 88,
89, 90, 91; Jorge de Mendoza and, 5
Spanish relations with as practical
necessity, 66, 74
and traditional marriage ties, 14, 15;
Spanish failure to honor, 15–16; ties
to colonists through, 15, 77–78
Necker, Louis, 13n22, 75n83
notaries, duties of, xi
Núñez, Pedro, 54, 61
Núñez Vela, Blasco, 64n55

officials, royal. *See also adelantados*
crown efforts to control, xiin1
need to justify actions in writing, 24
titles of, 10n18
Order of Santiago, 4
Orduña, Martín de, 8n15
Ortega, Juan de, 31, 31n4, 47, 48
Ortiz de Vergara, Francisco, 12
Ortiz de Zárate, Juan, 102, 102n5
Ortiz de Zárate, Juana, 102–3
Ortiz de Zárate y Mendieta, Diego, 102–3
Osorio, Juan, 5–6, 5n11, 30

Paraguay governorship, establishment
of, 103
Parguayan historiography, 1
Patronato Real, 68–69, 69n67
Pavón, Juan
on Abrego revolt, 63–64
and Cabeza de Vaca, loyalty to, 61
on Cabeza de Vaca, imprisonment of,
62–63
career of, 61, 62, 65
demands for justice by, 61–62, 65
imprisonment of, 61, 62
on Irala, misconduct by, 24, 61–65
letter to Martín de Agreda, 62–65;
notable features of, 24, 61–62

Pavón, Juan (cont'd)
    offices held by, 61, 62, 65
Payaguá people, 8, 45, 46–48, 58
Pérez, Catalina, 35
Pérez, Martín, 34
Peru, Viceroyalty of
    Chaves delegation to, 85n94, 87
    danger faced by mestizos in, 95
    Mendoza entrata from, 84–85, 84n92
    and monogamous marriage as issue,
        67–68, 68n65
    political authority over Río de la Plata,
        101, 101n1
    revolt in, 64, 64n55
Philip II (king of Spain), 36n15, 37,
    37n17, 102
Philip III (king of Spain), 103
Pineda, Elvira, 35
Pizarro, Francisco, 4n9, 32, 32n8, 33,
    64n55
Portugal
    and Brazil, discovery of, 3n6, 18, 18n29
    competition with Spain, 2–3
Portuguese traders, as guides and inter-
    preters, 18
Puerto, Francisco del, 20

Querandí people, 14

Ramírez, Melchor, 20
Ramos, Juan, 34
Rasquín, Jaime, 19
reducciones, gathering of Guaraní into,
    17–18
Relación de las cosas sucedidas en el Río
    de la Plata (Hernández), 2
religious conversion of natives. See also
    missionaries
    Andrada's efforts in, 67, 71–73
    Church rules on, 67n62, 72n75
    conflict with conquistadors' goals, 25
    eagerness for, 66, 67, 70, 72–73
    as purported goal of colonies, 65
Ribera, Hernando de, 20–22, 22n37
Río de la Plata. See also government of
    Río de la Plata
    absence of precious metals in, 101
    conquest of, homogeneity of indig-
        enous peoples and, 15
    early tenuous existence, xi, xii, 6, 23

economy of, 101
exploration and early colonization, 2–13
historians' limited attention to, 1
map of, xiii
poor soil of, 70, 101
rumors of riches in, 4, 5
splitting of (1607), 103
success of, as against the odds, 103
Río de Solís, 4. See also Río de la Plata
Rodríquez, Garci, 86, 90
Rojas, Diego de, 84n92
Romero, Gonzalo, 20
Roulet, Florencia, 15, 17
Ruiz Galán, Francisco
    entradas by, 7
    and Irala, struggle for power with, 8, 9,
        43, 46n28, 47
    as lieutenant governor of Buenos
        Aires, 6, 7, 31n6, 43, 46
    Pedro de Mendoza's instructions on,
        31–32, 33–34
    and search for Ayolas, 46
Rutre, Miguel de, 89

Saavedra, Hernandarias [Hernando
    Arias] de, 103, 103n7
Salazar de Espinosa, Juan de
    and Alonso Cabrera, 46n27
    and Asunción, founding of, 56
    and Ayolas, search for, 21–22, 45–46,
        47, 56
    entradas by, 7
    as lieutenant governor, 11, 31n5
    Pedro de Mendoza's instructions to, 30,
        31
    supporters of, 37
Sanabria, Diego de, as adelantado, 12n21
Sanabria, Juan de, 12n21, 19
San Buenaventura, Alonso de, 102n5
Sánchez, Mari, 35
Sancti Spíritus fort, xiii, 4, 6, 30, 84n92
San Fernando (port), 87
San Gabriel island, 50, 51
San Sebastián (port), 47, 57, 57n48
Santa Catalina island, 9, 10, 20, 21, 45,
    46n27, 49, 51
Santa Cruz de la Sierra, 17, 85n94, 102
Santa Fe, establishment of, 17
Santa María de la Asunción fort. See
    Asunción

Santa María del Buen Aire. *See* Buenos
  Aires
Schmidl [Schmidel; Schmidt], Ulrich,
  1–2, 6, 6n13
Second Council of Lima (1567-68), 68n65
Service, Elman, 36
sexual misbehavior with natives
  Andrada on, 74
  as contrary to colonial law, 76
  Irala and, González on, 76, 77, 80, 81,
    82, 88, 89, 90, 91
  Jorge de Mendoza and, 5
Sierra de la Plata
  failure to find, 13n22, 101
  legend of, 22, 22n37
  origin of legend of, 20n34
  search for, 4, 7, 9, 11–12, 57n48, 77
slavery, settlers' enslavement of natives,
  63, 74, 83–84, 87
  as illegal, 83n90
Southern passage, Spanish search for, 3–4
Spain, competition with Portugal, 2–3
Spanish crown
  complaints to: colonists' freedom to
    write, 24; inadequate compensation
    as common theme in, 36
  as head of Catholic Church in New
    World, 68–69, 68n66
  Irala as rebel against, González on, 79
  official's need to justify actions to, 24
  women as colonists, encouragement of,
    34–35
Strait of Magellan, discovery of, 3–4

Tamacocíes people, 87
Timbú people, 14, 41, 56, 84

tithe, controversy over collection of,
  97–98
Tordesillas, Treaty of (1494), 3
Torres de Vera y Aragón, Juan, 103
Tuer, Dorothy, 1, 13–14n24, 16, 17, 21,
  22n37
Tupí people, 13, 14

Vadillo, Catalina de, 35
Valderas, Juan de, 22
Vásquez de Orejón, Juan, 5n11
Venegas, García de, 50–51, 50n34, 55, 60
Vera, Francisco de, 54
Vergara, Ortiz de, 101–2
Vicente, Martín de, 91
Villa Rica del Espíritu Santo, 17
Villavicencio, Francisco de, 54, 61
Vitoria, Francisco de, 68n66

*Warhafftige und liebliche Beschreibung
  erstlicher furnemen Indianischen
  Landtschafften und Insulen*
  (Schmidl), 1–2
women, native. *See* native women
women colonists. *See also* Guevara,
  Isabel de
  number of, 35
  roles of, 34–35; crown's promotion of,
    34–35; Isabel Guevara on, 23–24, 35,
    41–42

Xarae people, 22
Xarayes people, 53

latin american originals

Series Editor | Matthew Restall

This series features primary source texts on colonial and nineteenth-century Latin America, translated into English, in slim, accessible, affordable editions that also make scholarly contributions. Most of these sources are being published in English for the first time and represent an alternative to the traditional texts on early Latin America. The initial focus is on the conquest period in sixteenth-century Spanish America, but subsequent volumes include Brazil and examine later centuries. The series features archival documents and printed sources originally in Spanish, Portuguese, Latin, and various Native American languages. The contributing authors are historians, anthropologists, art historians, and scholars of literature.

Matthew Restall is Edwin Erle Sparks Professor of Colonial Latin American History, Anthropology, and Women's Studies, and Co-Director of Latina/o, Latin American, and Caribbean Studies, at the Pennsylvania State University. He is an editor of *Ethnohistory*.

Board of Editorial Consultants
J. Michael Francis (chair)
Jane G. Landers | Kris Lane
Laura E. Matthew | Martin Austin Nesvig

Titles in Print

*Invading Colombia: Spanish Accounts of the
Gonzalo Jiménez de Quesada Expedition of Conquest* (LAO 1)
J. Michael Francis

Invading Guatemala: Spanish, Nahua, and Maya Accounts of the Conquest Wars (LAO 2)
Matthew Restall and Florine G. L. Asselbergs

*The Conquest on Trial: Carvajal's "Complaint of the Indians
in the Court of Death"* (LAO 3)
Carlos A. Jáuregui

*Defending the Conquest: Bernardo de Vargas Machuca's
"Defense and Discourse of the Western Conquests"* (LAO 4)
Edited by Kris Lane and translated by Timothy F. Johnson

*Forgotten Franciscans: Works from an Inquisitional Theorist, a Heretic,
and an Inquisitional Deputy* (LAO 5)
Martin Austin Nesvig

*Gods of the Andes: An Early Jesuit Account of Inca Religion
and Andean Christianity* (LAO 6)
Sabine Hyland

Of Cannibals and Kings: Primal Anthropology in the Americas (LAO 7)
Neil L. Whitehead

Translated Christianities: Nahuatl and Maya Religious Texts (LAO 8)
Mark Z. Christensen